Gaining a Face

Gaining a Face:
The Romanticism of C.S. Lewis

By

James Prothero and Donald T. Williams

CAMBRIDGE
SCHOLARS
P U B L I S H I N G

Gaining a Face: The Romanticism of C.S. Lewis,
by James Prothero and Donald T. Williams

This book first published 2013

Cambridge Scholars Publishing

12 Back Chapman Street, Newcastle upon Tyne, NE6 2XX, UK

British Library Cataloguing in Publication Data
A catalogue record for this book is available from the British Library

ISBN (10): 1-4438-5235-X, ISBN (13): 978-1-4438-5235-7

To
Walter Hooper

TABLE OF CONTENTS

ACKNOWLEDGEMENTS

We want to thank all our friends at the Southern California C.S. Lewis Society who heard various parts of this book in its infant stages at two separate summer workshops. We also want to thank Dr. Jane Hipolito, the dean of Barfield scholars, for her invaluable insight and feedback on the sections pertaining to Owen Barfield.

All citations are in the Chicago Manual of Style format, with the exception of citations of books by C.S. Lewis, which are so numerous to differentiate, even by date, that we have resorted to the following abbreviations for the sake of clarity:

Key to Abbreviations of titles by C.S. Lewis:

AL	*Allegory of Love*
AM	*Abolition of Man*
CLCSL1	*The Collected Letters of C.S. Lewis*, Volume One
CLCSL2	*The Collected Letters of C.S. Lewis*, Volume Two
CLCSL3	*The Collected Letters of C.S. Lewis*, Volume Three
CP	*Collected Poems*
CR	*Christian Reflections*
DI	*The Discarded Image*
FL	*The Four Loves*
GID	*God in the Dock*
GO	*A Grief Observed*
HHB	*The Horse and His Boy*
LB	*The Last Battle*
LM	*Letters to Malcolm, Chiefly on Prayer*
LWW	*The Lion, The Witch and the Wardrobe*
MN	*The Magician's Nephew*
OHEL	*Oxford History of English Literature: English Literature in the Sixteenth Century Excluding Drama*
OOW	*Of Other Worlds*
OS	*C.S. Lewis On Stories*
PC	*Prince Caspian*
P	*Perelandra*

PP	*Problem of Pain*
PPL	*Preface to Paradise Lost*
SBJ	*Surprised by Joy*
SC	*The Silver Chair*
SL	*Selected Letters*
SLE	*Selected Literary Essays*
TWHF	*Till We Have Faces*
VDT	*The Voyage of the Dawn Treader*
WG	*The Weight of Glory and Other Addresses*

PREFACE:
ROMANTICISM AND C.S. LEWIS

Over the years since 1950 and the publication of *The Lion, The Witch and The Wardrobe*, or perhaps since 1942 and the publication of *The Screwtape Letters*, the reading public in America and the United Kingdom has been aware of the Romantic aspect of the vision of C.S. Lewis. Before that time he was a little known tutor in English at Magdalen College, Oxford, and Christian apologist to be heard in the war years over the BBC. The broadcast talks that later became *Mere Christianity* revealed a mind given to metaphorical thinking and analogy; this chap on the BBC going on about religion definitely had a vivid imagination and the gift of communicating with that imagination. But until *Screwtape* and the Narnia Chronicles, the full depth and scope, and the sheer lushness of that vision was unrevealed to the public. "Jack" Lewis was first a believer in reason, and also in revelation. He was tutored in a hard school of logic by W.T. Kirkpatrick. His final transition to belief in the factual nature of the claims of Christ is well documented in *Surprised by Joy*. But as the autobiography details, Lewis was taken with the experience he called "joy." That fact has been already well-documented and will not be the focus of this study. What we wish to do here is to focus on the entirety of Lewis's Romanticism.

Before we discuss the specifics of Lewis's Romantic side, we must address two thorny issues. The first problem in claiming a Romantic aspect for a writer like Lewis, who did not live in the four decades encompassing and following the French Revolution, is defining the term "Romantic." There really isn't any agreed upon definition amongst Romantic scholars that I could appeal to. And there is rather a cottage industry of scholars proposing definitions of Romanticism and disagreeing with one another. For the purposes of this study, we will use the following definition which I have developed over years of teaching Romanticism in the classroom. Students don't care about scholarly controversy. They need something concrete. I find the following works.

Romanticism, especially the British form, is a rough grouping of several concepts that came out of the response in Britain to the French Revolution. To touch on at least a couple of these concepts in the 1798-

1832 period generally gets a writer defined as Romantic. It is not necessary for a writer to claim all these traits to be considered Romantic, so that though Byron may only claim one or two of these, Percy Shelley claims far more. Jane Austen, though she wrote in this period, claims none, and is generally not considered Romantic.

The first and central concept is the intrinsic value of the imagination. Coleridge is famous for his theories of the imagination and all the writers of this period have their own ideas on the imagination, its importance and its nature.

The second concept is the intrinsic value of nature. Here again, there is tremendous variety of definition here from Keats to Wordsworth to Byron. But this is fairly universal to all the Romantics. Though we have a range from Coleridge's theistic transcendentalism to Shelley's atheism to Keats' agnosticism, the Romantics universally find some level of spiritual value to the beauty of nature. This concept gave birth to the conservation movement and our propensity to set land aside for national parks and monuments.

The third concept is the special character of children. The Romantics really popularized the concept of children as being born innocent and requiring a literature all their own, as well as the concept that we would now call "child development." This difference in thought led many of the Romantics and some Victorians after them to oppose child labor. Blake is well known for his portrayal of the corruption of childhood innocence by the industrial revolution. Blake felt that we are born innocent and go on to (notice I did not say "progress") experience. Shelley and Wordsworth played with the notion that children were closest to God, having been in his presence just before birth. To see the world as a child is to see it more clearly.

The fourth concept is the intrinsic value of the common man. This is a concept directly a result of the American and French Revolutions, tied closely to Locke's principals of government and the veneration of the will of the masses in the French Revolution. Wordsworth evoked this in *The Lyrical Ballads*, with his portrayal of simple country folk.

The fifth concept I will use is the sense of balance in the concept of good and evil. Blake talks of the marriage of heaven and hell. Whatever else he may have meant by that, it is typical of his sense that the good in the world, usually associated with childhood and innocence, and the evil in the world, usually but not always associated with experience, are in balance. Of course, Blake's concept is more complex than my gloss here, and his concept of evil is very complex indeed. But the point is that he sees these forces in balance. Wordsworth too will portray sorrow and joy and try to balance them as the various narrators in *The Excursion* attempt to do. This contrasts the twentieth century view that the presence of evil negates good.

The sixth and final concept we will use here is the Romantic fascination with utopias, perfect worlds: finding them, building them, and exploring the vision of the perfect world. Romantics are in a search for paradise, or Heaven, or perhaps Heaven on Earth. Coleridge and Southey participated in the ill-fated utopia they were going to build in the wilds of Pennsylvania called "Pantisocracy."

The second thorny problem is as we look at Wordsworth and MacDonald and subsequently Lewis, and the divine transcendence they find in nature, we become aware that they are not the first to find the divine in nature. Going back to the writing of Psalm 19 at the very least, humanity has seen the creator in creation. However, the Romantic age was to a large degree a reaction to the rationalistic 18th century before, which tended to see nature as a deistic clock. There is in these four decades re-visioning of the view of nature that brings a new emphasis to man's view of nature. Wordsworth made his reputation as the "poet of nature" in this respect, and in this study we will be looking at the way that Wordsworth's vision grows and changes as it passes from him to MacDonald to Lewis. Combined with the heightened respect for the imagination, the Romantics brought a very different quality and a resurgent energy to the concept of nature, that is commonly recognized and not the subject of this study.

Thus in this study, we are going to follow the manifestations in the works of Lewis of: 1) the beautiful, especially as it shows itself in natural imagery, what Lewis calls "sensibility to natural objects", and of the transcendental view of nature; 2) Lewis's utopianism expressed in the focus on Heaven, getting to Heaven and the imagery of Heaven that works its way into his fiction; 3) the childlike state that is found in MacDonald's fiction and makes its way into Lewis and how Lewis adopts this childlike clarity in his own view of literature. These three features, after Lewis's central concern with joy, are the most prominent marks of the Romantic side of his thought and fiction.

Lastly, it would be unjust not to acknowledge R.J. Reilly's excellent 1971 book, *Romantic Religion: A Study of Barfield, Lewis, Williams and Tolkien*, which is full of shrewd insight on the subject. However, as insightful as Reilly has been on Lewis, there are elements originating in the thought of Wordsworth and MacDonald, specifically in Lewis's imagery, his sense of paradox, his characterization and his stance toward criticism, that Reilly does not explore to the depth we will do so here. We will examine how the Romantic sense permeates Lewis's thought over a century after the Romantic period, and how that resurgent Romanticism offers an alternative to the patterns of thought that began with Modernism, and creates a strong opposition to the prevailing trends.

CHAPTER ONE

BEAUTY, WORDSWORTH, AND LEWIS

Something has always bothered me about the English Romantic poets.

I fell in love with them as an adolescent reader because they were such an oasis of beauty in the arid deserts of Neoclassicism that preceded them and of Modernism that followed. (I've since realized that I was not being quite fair to the eighteenth century, though I remain unreconciled to much of the twentieth—but those are other stories.) The Romantics did not reduce Nature either to the perfect clockwork operating by universal laws of the preceding century, nor to the grinding, indifferent, impersonal machine of the following one. To them she was a living being larger than they were who enabled them to experience humility, wonder, and adoration—responses that made the Romantics, to my mind then as now, more fully human than people in whom those feelings are atrophied or absent.

Like Wordsworth in "Tintern Abbey," I aspired to have "an eye made quiet by the power / Of harmony, and the deep power of joy," believing that only thus could I "see into the life of things" (ll. 47-49, Wordsworth 1988, 164). And like Wordsworth in the same poem, I thought that I had felt

A presence that disturbs me with the joy
Of elevated thoughts; a sense sublime
Of something far more deeply interfused,
Whose dwelling is the light of setting suns,
And the round ocean, and the living air,
And the blue sky, and in the mind of man:
A motion and a spirit that impels
All thinking things, all objects of all thought,
And rolls through all things. (ll. 93-102, Wordsworth 1988, 164)

This was a good place to start, the beginning of a Quest to last a lifetime. Wordsworth apparently thought so too: Renwick observes of

"Tintern Abbey" that the poet "spent the rest of his life expanding, glossing, commenting upon that poem" (158).

The Problems

So what was the problem? There were two. First, such feelings were inspiring, but they could only take one so far. Was this Presence that disturbed us with elevated thoughts a personal God? Something like the Force of Star Wars? A Platonic Idea? A mere personification of Nature (whatever that meant)? A sheer illusion? Nature gave you a sense that there was *Something* behind her that made you want to think her more than just atoms in motion, but she couldn't tell you much more than that; and this vague Something could fully satisfy neither Religion nor Philosophy. Nature made you feel like she was helping you to ask the right question, but she couldn't give you the answer to it. She gave you some very interesting hunches, but no more—and no sure way to confirm the validity even of the hunches.

Second, even the hunches tended to fade if they remained no more than that. Nature and her beauty could get you started on the Quest, but she couldn't sustain you in it, much less complete it. Wordsworth felt this problem acutely in his "Ode on Intimations of Immortality." The cataracts and mountains used to haunt him like a passion, but while he still loves them and still appreciates their beauty on some level, he has to that "The things which I have seen I now can see no more" (l. 9, Wordsworth 1988, 460). His own loss of vision would be bad enough, but it seemed to be more than that: "There hath passed away a glory from the earth" (l. 18). And so he cries out in a desperation like Paul's "O wretched man that I am" (Rom. 7:24), "Whither is fled the visionary gleam? / Where is it now, the glory and the dream?" (ll. 56-7, Wordsworth 1988, 460).

The first problem could be put on the back burner, but this one was immediately pressing. The young man still haunted by passion felt quite threatened by the promise of losing it, and he had the nagging dread that Wordsworth knew what he was talking about. Worse, the poet's attempt to cope with his own loss smelled strongly like a blatant orgy of rationalization:

> Though nothing can bring back the hour
> Of splendour in the grass, of glory in the flower;
> We will grieve not, rather find
> Strength in what remains behind:
> In the primal sympathy
> Which having been must ever be;

In the soothing thoughts that spring
Out of human suffering;
In the faith that looks through death,
In years that bring the philosophic mind. (ll. 177-86, Wordsworth 1988, 461)

The problem with these lines is that the poet's more "mature" stoic resignation does not necessarily connect with or logically flow from the stimulus that supposedly gave rise to it. To cut one's losses is the gambit of the Poker Player, not the Nature Mystic. One ought to sympathize with suffering humanity anyway, whether one has ever been passionate about cataracts or not, and whether that former passion is moderating over time or not. And it takes more than some vague, elevating Presence to explain how any thoughts arising from human suffering can be "soothing," or to be the ground of any "faith that looks through death" to find a justified hope of something good, as opposed to oblivion, on the other side. If this is the "philosophic mind" that the years bring, we would be wiser to remain naïve but impassioned adolescents.

Keats, the greatest verbal craftsman of the Romantics, had his own way of arousing and disappointing the same hope. His Grecian Urn had told him that "'Beauty is truth, truth beauty.'—That is all / Ye know on earth, and all ye need to know" (ll. 49-50, Keats 1970, 210). Endless attempts have been made to figure out what Keats meant by this assertion. Those scholars are no doubt right who try to limit its scope: Beauty is truth "is the most important thing men need to know *concerning the subject at hand* (the relation of art to life)" (Patterson 1970, 180-81; cf. Wasserman 1964, 138). That is, some such interpretation most successfully renders a statement that makes sense. Yet Keats' words, like quicksilver, refuse to be contained by such analysis. His equation is not the "most important" thing we need to know; it is *all*. Surely it expresses at least the Wordsworthian hope that beauty is not just a mere epiphenomenon, a Yeatsian "spume that plays / upon a ghostly paradigm of things," an appearance, or a mere subjective response on our part, but somehow connects us to the deepest Reality—to Truth.

Now this would be a wonderful truth to know, if we could know it. But is Nature capable of telling us that it is so? Or are she and the truth she seems to offer us merely the occasion for our own wishful thinking, an exercise in selectivity that simply turns a blind eye to the fact that her beauty somehow manages to coexist with a certain cruelty and indifference, red in tooth and claw? Nature can raise this question, but by herself she cannot answer it.

One way of testing our beliefs is to try to live by them, and Keats makes a noble attempt to live by his. In doing so he illustrates C. S. Lewis's observation:

> We do not merely want to see beauty, though, God knows, even that is bounty enough. We want something else which can hardly be put into words—to be united with the beauty we see, to pass into it, to receive it into ourselves, to bathe in it, to become part of it. (WG 12)

The poetic depiction of this attempt is the "Ode to a Nightingale." The bird is the personification of a beauty that seems to transcend "the weariness, the fever, and the fret" (l. 23) of human life. Eschewing the intoxication proffered by Bacchus as a way of getting there that can produce only illusion at best, Keats strains to fly to the bird "on the viewless wings of poesy" (l.33). But all his efforts serve only to highlight the contrast between the ethereal immortality of the bird's song and the clod-like dullness and darkness of his own state. His attempt to be one with beauty through poetic imagination is inspiring and admirable, but it is also an admitted failure:

> Forlorn! The very word is like a bell
> To toll me back from thee to my sole self!
> Adieu! The fancy cannot cheat so well
> As she is famed to do, deceiving elf. (ll. 71-4)

He ends up, like the knight at arms in his "Belle Dame sans Merci," on the cold hillside, called out of himself by the song of the bird, but unable to answer the call and not even certain of what has happened: "Do I wake or sleep?" (l. 80, Keats 1970, 207-9).

The English Romantics then show us that the beauty of Nature raises questions it cannot answer and inspires hopes it cannot fulfill. They start us on our Quest but cannot see us to the end of it. We must be grateful for what they give us, but we must also ultimately go beyond them or else fall back into cynicism, naturalism, and despair. So the pressing question becomes whether there is anyone who can supply the missing pieces to the puzzle. C. S. Lewis offers some pieces that are at least worthy of our consideration.

Lewis and Beauty

Lewis invites us to read his own quest in Wordsworthian terms by choosing as the title of his autobiography a phrase from one of

Wordsworth's sonnets: "surprised by joy." Lewis used *joy* (along with the German word *sehnsucht*) as a technical term for the stab of romantic longing generated by beauty. More cosmopolitan in his tastes than Wordsworth, Lewis could receive it not just from Nature (the Castlereagh Hills) but also from literature (Norse mythology), music (Wagner), or art (a toy garden made by his brother on the lid of a biscuit tin and brought into the nursery). Indeed, he records, Warnie's toy garden "was the first beauty I ever knew," not important at the moment but "important in memory" (SBJ 7). For a few years later, "There suddenly arose in me without warning, and as if from a depth not of years but of centuries, that memory of the earlier morning at the Old House when my brother had brought his toy garden into the nursery" (16). The memory filled him with an acute longing. What did he want? Not the biscuit lid nor his own past, but *something* not yet nameable that was represented by the remembered beauty. He could only describe the experience as an "unsatisfied desire which is itself more desirable than any other satisfaction" (18). And this experience of Wordsworthian haunting became nothing less than "the central story of my life" (17).

Like Wordsworth, Lewis was haunted by beauty. Like Keats, he wanted the truth; but, unlike Keats, his hardnosed logical thinking, learned from "the Old Knock," his tutor William T. Kirkpatrick, was not making any facile identification of truth with beauty possible. By his adolescence he had reached the point where he cared only about Balder and the great myths but believed only in atoms in motion. Thus he found like Wordsworth that the glory was passing away, only he did not have the comfort of Wordsworth's rationalizations of that passing to console him. And so by early manhood he could say, "As for Joy, I labeled it 'aesthetic experience' and talked much about it under that name and said it was very 'valuable.' But it came very seldom and when it came it didn't amount to much" (SBJ 205). Had the story ended there, Lewis would have had little to add to what we had already learned from Wordsworth and Keats.

But of course the story does not end there. Lewis was running into Christian writers like George MacDonald and Christian friends like Neville Coghill, Hugo Dyson, and J. R. R. Tolkien, who were forcing him to reconsider whether atoms in motion were a sufficient explanation for the world as he experienced it. His journey from Atheism to Idealism to Theism to Christianity is fully narrated, literally in *Surprised by Joy* and allegorically in *The Pilgrim's Regress*, and it is outside the scope of this study to repeat it here. Our question is rather, given that Lewis became convinced that God exists and has revealed himself in Jesus Christ, what effect did this conversion have on his relationship to beauty, or, as he put it, to "joy"?

It had the effect, interestingly, of reversing the disappearance of the glory from the earth. Let Lewis tell the story in his own words:

> I cannot indeed complain, like Wordsworth, that the visionary gleam has passed away. I believe (if the thing were at all worth recording) that the old stab, the old bitter-sweet, has come to me as often and as sharply since my conversion as at any time of my life whatever. But I now know that the experience, considered as a state of my own mind, had never had the kind of importance I once gave it. It was valuable only as a pointer to something other and outer. While that other was in doubt, the pointer naturally loomed large in my thoughts. When we are lost in the woods the sight of a signpost is a great matter. He who first sees it cries, "Look!" The whole party gathers round and stares. But when we have found the road and are passing signposts every few miles, we shall not stop and stare. They will encourage us and we shall be grateful to the authority who set them up. But we shall not stop and stare, or not much; not on this road, though their pillars are of silver and their lettering of gold. "We would be at Jerusalem." (SBJ 238)

Beauty as a Second Thing

What is happening here? On the surface, it seems paradoxical that a demotion of beauty in importance should lead to a renewed and greater appreciation of it. Yet Lewis came to understand this paradox as the exemplification of a pattern basic to all of life. It was in fact "a universal law": "Every preference of a small good to a great, or a partial good to a total good, involves the loss of the small or partial good for which the sacrifice was made. . . . You can't get second things by putting them first; you can get second things only by putting first things first" (GID, "First and Second Things" 280).

This law is certainly widely true. If you try to hit home runs, you just strike out and pop up a lot. If you swing the bat with good form and keep your eye on the ball, you hit line drives, some of which may go over the fence. If you try too hard to make friends you may just push people away. If you care about others more than yourself, you may end up with some very good friends. If you put all your hopes for meaning into subjective experiences of beauty, they may leave you empty. If you pursue the truth and find it, you just might get beauty thrown in. That, in any case, is how Lewis interpreted his own experience.

Now, another way of confirming our beliefs is by their fruitfulness. By fruitfulness, philosophers of science do not mean utilitarianism, but rather the way in which a belief that leads you to other true beliefs tends to be confirmed by that fact (Polanyi 1964, 147). So it is significant that Lewis's conversion to Christianity helped him to see the very principle that illumined his experience. Corbin Scott Carnell explains that

> Many writers became disillusioned with Romanticism in the twentieth century precisely because they expected too much of it. Lewis retained his faith in the basic validity of Romantic literature because he believed it was compatible with a Christian ontology. The sense of nostalgia cannot be valued for itself, at least not for long. *Sehnsucht* has genuine meaning only in an ontology which has a place for it. (158-9).

Christian faith, in other words, provides a basis for distinguishing first and second things. If God exists and created the world, then there is an objective hierarchy of goodness that begins with and proceeds from the basic distinction between the Creator and the creation (Williams, "The Mind is its own Place"). This distinction gives us a basis for avoiding what Meilander calls "the sweet poison of the false infinite." He sees it as one of Lewis's most central themes that "To be fully human involves a certain stance toward the things of creation: delighting in things without seeking our security in them" (8). If, on the other hand, the world just exists on its own or evolved by chance, then there is no basis for such a distinction, for everything just is, and all hierarchical rankings are arbitrary.

We are back to living out our beliefs as a way of testing them. Can we really live as if there is no valid distinction to be made between first and second things? Lewis's conclusion was "no." And that "no" seemed to explain the difference between his experience of beauty and Wordsworth's.

Lewis wrote a lot about this insight as related specifically to the experience of beauty, not only in his autobiography but also in expository works like *The Four Loves*, where he makes the first and second things even more explicit in Christian terms. "We can't get through; not that way. We must make a detour—leave the hills and the woods and go back to our studies, to the church, to our Bibles, to our knees. Otherwise the love of nature is beginning to turn into a nature religion" (FL 38). The reason why turning Nature into a religion is a mistake is that "Nature cannot satisfy the desires she arouses nor answer theological questions nor sanctify us. . . . But the love of her has been a valuable and, for some people, an indispensable initiation" (39). If God is God and Nature his creature, this is just what we should expect.

> In fact, those who allow no more than this to the love of nature seem to be those who retain it. . . . Nature 'dies' on those who try to live for a love of

nature. Coleridge ended by being insensible to her; Wordsworth, by lamenting that the glory had passed away. Say your prayers in a garden early, steadfastly ignoring the dew, the birds, and the flowers, and you will come away overwhelmed by its freshness and joy; go there to be overwhelmed and, after a certain age, nothing will happen to you. (39).

We also have this, from *The Weight of Glory*:

> Our commonest expedient is to call it beauty and behave as if that had settled the matter. . . . [But] the books or the music in which we thought the beauty was located will betray us if we trust to them; it was not in them, it only came through them, and what came through them was longing. These things—the beauty, the memory of our own past—are good images of what we really desire; but if they are mistaken for the thing itself, they turn into dumb idols, breaking the hearts of their worshippers. (WG 4-5)

All right, then. Treating Nature and her beauty as a Second Thing, as a creature of God rather than as an end in itself, allows Lewis to have both God *and* beauty. At least, that is his experience as he reports it. If we grant this truth, then, what else follows from it?

The Objectivity of Beauty

One further conclusion is the objectivity of beauty. The very existence of first and second things flows from the existence of a good creator God who expressed His character in His creation. If this is the case, then the very consideration that keeps beauty from being a first thing also makes it a real thing. If a personal God values His creation, then the values He has placed in it are really there, waiting for our response and not merely caused by it. Lewis is very much aware of the contradictions that ensue from denying this idea, as he explains in *Abolition of Man*:

> Gaius and Titius comment as follows: "when the man said *That is sublime*, he appeared to be making a remark about the waterfall. . . . Actually . . . he was not making a remark about the waterfall, but a remark about his own feelings. What he was saying was really *I have feelings associated in my mind with the word 'Sublime,'* or shortly, *I have sublime feelings.*" (AM 14; cf. Williams 2006, 26-39)

But of course that is not what the man is intending to say at all. And if we pretend it is, we will soon be subjectivizing his statements about the moral law and even the laws of logic as well—with the result that we will then not be able to think about anything at all (cf. the argument from reason in *Miracles*; "The Poison of Subjectivism"; etc). The alternative is to believe "the universe to be such that certain emotional reactions on our part could be either congruous or incongruous to it . . . that objects did not merely receive, but could *merit*, our approval or disapproval, our reverence, or our contempt" (AM 25). The doctrine of objective value holds that "certain attitudes are really true, and others really false, to the kind of thing the universe is and the kind of things we are." This means that "to call children delightful or old men venerable is not simply to record a psychological fact about our own parental or filial emotions at the moment, but to recognize a quality which *demands* a certain response from us whether we make it or not" (29). It follows then, to return to the topic of beauty, that

> There is no reason why our reaction to a beautiful landscape should not be the response, however humanly blurred and partial, to something that is really there. The idea of a wholly mindless and valueless universe has to be abandoned at one point—i.e., as regards logic: after that, there is no telling at how many other points it will be defeated nor how great the reversal of our nineteenth century philosophy must finally be. (CR "*De Futilitate*" 71)

Lewis's analysis of the psychology of love and desire in *The Four Loves* is consistent with this perspective. Some pleasures—like a drink of cold water—are dependent on our subjective state or our need. We only really appreciate the water if we are thirsty. But then there are also what Lewis calls "Pleasures of Appreciation," which are not dependent on our subjective condition but "make us feel that something has not merely gratified our senses in fact but claimed our appreciation by right." A person passing a garden planted with sweet peas "does not simply enjoy, he feels that this fragrance somehow deserves to be enjoyed. He would blame himself if he went past inattentive and undelighted. It would be blockish, insensitive" (29). He continues,

> In the Appreciative pleasures, even at their lowest, and even more as they grow up into the full appreciation of all beauty, we get something we can hardly help calling love and hardly help calling disinterested, towards the object itself. It is the feeling which would make a man unwilling to deface a great picture even if he were the last man left alive and himself about to die; which makes us glad of unspoiled forests that we shall never see; which makes us anxious that the garden or bean-field should continue to exist. We do not merely like the things; we pronounce them, in a momentarily God-like sense, "very good." (32)

In doing so, Lewis thinks we are recognizing a real truth and seconding, as it were, God's pronouncement of Nature's goodness in Genesis.

The Function of Beauty

Also flowing from Lewis's basic insight is a perspective on the function of beauty. In his autobiography he called it a signpost pointing us to God. This also follows inevitably from the doctrine of creation. What God has made reflects the nature of its Maker. It does so imperfectly after the Fall, but the reflection, while dimmed and distorted in certain ways, has not been erased. So truth when we find it in the world is a reflection of God's mind, goodness of His character, and beauty of his glory, impressed into the very fabric of what He has made (see Kreeft 2008, 23-5). This Christian ontology allows beauty to function as the signpost Lewis discovered it to be, and the response unleashed by it not only prevents Wordsworth's loss of vision but even heightens the vision and the longing. "Gratitude exclaims, very properly, 'How good of God to give me this.' Adoration says, 'What must be the quality of that Being whose far-off and momentary coruscations are like this!' One's mind runs back up the sunbeam to the sun" (LM 90).

Beauty pursued for its own sake dulls and disappoints eventually. Beauty received as a pointer to the God of creation leads to worship. "Need-love cries to God from our poverty; Gift-love longs to serve, or even suffer for, God; Appreciative love says, 'We give thee thanks for thy great glory'" (FL 33). In other words, if beauty does not lead us back to its source in the creator God, it fails of its purpose. We may admire the intricacy of the Message, but we have not *read* it. Consequently, we eventually lose interest. Beauty read as a sign stimulates us to praise, not just of the beautiful object, but also of its Maker. "Of every created thing I praise, I should say, 'In some way, in its unique way, like Him who made it.' Thus up from the garden to the Gardener, from the sword to the Smith. To the life-giving Life and the Beauty that makes beautiful" (GO 50).

Conclusion

This chapter does not claim to have proved from the phenomenon of beauty that God exists or that Jesus is His Son. Many more factors go into the decision whether or not to believe those propositions than we were able to address here. What it does try to do is to elucidate one aspect of C. S. Lewis's testimony, his personal witness to the existence of that God. One way of testing our beliefs is to see if they hold up when we try to live by them. Another way is by their fruitfulness, i.e., the fact that they lead to further insights that are also confirmed by life. Lewis found that his conversion to Christianity solved for him certain problems of aesthetics that the Romantic poets were unable to solve, and that what Carnell aptly calls the "Christian ontology" was the key to that solution. Lewis's experience was that at these points his life tended to confirm his Christian faith, and his writings give his testimony to that confirmation.

The Romantics cared about beauty but lacked a sufficient grounding for it to make it fully meaningful. Wordsworth found that it slipped through his fingers, and Keats ultimately failed to make its relationship to truth anything more than wishful thinking. Lewis discovered that his conversion to Christian faith had the effect of making beauty a Second Thing. "Lewis cautioned that beauty was the sign and not the signifier and that to make it a 'first thing' was to crush and lose it" (Prothero 1998, 94). Making beauty secondary to God ironically exalts beauty rather than erasing it because it enables us not only to believe in God but also in the ultimate goodness of "a world which God has inseminated with all sorts of realities that carry their hidden winsome reminders of Himself" (Kilby 1964, 41).

Lewis also realized that this move of making beauty a Second Thing ironically not only led to the preservation of his experience of beauty but also to an understanding of it that makes Keats' affirmation of its relation to truth meaningful. We want Keats to be right; we want beauty to be more than just a subjective appearance. As Kilby says, we do not want "truth and beauty, or truth decorated with beauty, or truth illustrated by the beautiful phrase, or truth in a 'beautiful setting'" (Kilby 1961, 20). We want something more whole than that. But how can we find it?

Lewis's stress on the objectivity of beauty hints at its relation to truth, and his defense of its objectivity in *The Abolition of Man* is explicitly related to the objectivity of goodness and truth as well. The unity of beauty, truth, and goodness cannot be found within the horizon of temporal experience, i.e., in Nature, but only in God. Finite Nature is a prism that breaks up the light of the infinite God into the distinguished Transcendentals. Only when we see that can we see Von Balthasar's wonderful vision in which "Beauty . . . dances as an uncontained splendour around the double constellation of the true and the good and their inseparable relation to one another" (18). If truth is the reflection of God's mind, goodness of His character, and beauty of His glory in the world He has made, then any of them can led us back to the Source. Lewis learned, and can teach us, to follow all three paths.

This then is Lewis's testimony: Accepting the Christian ontology was unexpectedly fruitful in that it led to a view of beauty that enhanced and enabled a life of appreciation for beauty by supplying the missing pieces in the attempts of the Romantics to lead such a life. Beauty understood thus makes every experience of beauty one more bit of support for that world view. "This probative energy silently shouts out from its radiant form: 'This is so; this is real, authentic, good, and true'" (Dubay 1999, 23).

We are surrounded by Signposts, if Lewis was right. Was he? Can he help us learn to read them? For what it's worth, not only my exposition here but also my own experience of such things causes me to answer, "Yes."

CHAPTER TWO

THE ROMANTIC ROOTS,
WORDSWORTH AND COLERIDGE

Lewis was far clearer about joy and beauty than Wordsworth; in a sense, he finishes what Wordsworth left unfinished. I have often wondered if Wordsworth, who arrived at orthodoxy late in life, and was a first rate mind, worked his way to the same conclusions Lewis did. However, there is no evidence for this either way. Wordsworth in some sense, as I will show, shared the same role in Victorian society that Lewis did in twentieth century Britain, as a spokesman for faith. But Wordsworth was reluctant to pronounce on the specifics of faith, unlike Lewis. Most accounts credit Wordsworth as being a pantheist early in his career. However, the record doesn't bear that out. Beginning with the question of what Wordsworth did believe, I wish to explore how that concept of romanticized faith is transmitted through Coleridge, MacDonald, Chesterton and Barfield, and ultimately to Lewis.

Wordsworth's Alleged Pantheism

It is commonly held that Wordsworth in his younger years was a pantheist. I have heard this now in more than one lecture and conference. And yet, when I examine the record, I find something far more complex actually occurred. In order for us to understand Wordsworth's move to Christianity, we need to be clear about where he was moving from. The passage most often cited to prove Wordsworth's alleged pantheism is from "Tintern Abbey":

And I have felt
A presence that disturbs me with the joy
Of elevated thoughts; a sense sublime
Of something far more deeply interfused,
Whose dwelling is the light of setting suns,
And the round ocean and the living air,

And the blue sky, and in the mind of man;
A motion and a spirit, that impels
All thinking things, all objects of all thought,
And rolls through all things. (ll. 93-102 Wordsworth 1988, 164)

The lines are incredibly vague. They could be made to read pantheism, or a vague theism, or just Wordsworth's sense of things as he felt them in his heart. He is writing this, we know from the full title, "Lines Composed a Few Miles Above Tintern Abbey, on Revisiting the Banks of the Wye during a Tour, July 13, 1798" on July 13, 1798. He is staying with Dorothy at the house of his printer, Joseph Cottle in Bristol, and taking a day trip with Dorothy across the Bristol Channel and up the valley of the Wye. He is in Bristol because he, Dorothy, and Coleridge are overseeing the final printing of *Lyrical Ballads*, which they hope will produce enough money to enable them to travel to Germany. By the end of the year, Wordsworth and Dorothy are in Goslar, Germany, and he is writing the first version of *The Prelude*. In or before February of 1799, on the back of a manuscript of the poem "Peter Bell," he writes:

Such consciousness I deem but accidents,
Relapses from the one interior life
That lives in all things, sacred from the touch
Of that false secondary power by which
In weakness we create distinctions, then
Believe that all our puny boundaries are thing
Which we perceive, and not which we have made—
In which all beings live with God, themselves
Are God, existing in one mighty whole,
As undistinguishable as the cloudless east
At noon is from the cloudless west, when all
The hemisphere is one cerulean blue.
(in Jonathan Wordsworth, et al 1979, ll. 9-21, 496)

This is clearly pantheistic, unlike the lines in "Tintern Abbey." However, Wordsworth *does not publish these lines.* They were found by scholars in the twentieth century on the back of this manuscript of "Peter Bell." Wordsworth suppresses these lines. Later that year he completes the first version of *The Prelude*, the so-called "Two-Part *Prelude* of 1799." Sometime around May 1st of 1799, Wordsworth and Dorothy are back in England at the home of the Hutchinsons. Though he does not publish it, Wordsworth is pretty much finished with the Two-Part *Prelude*.

In that Two-Part *Prelude* is the stolen boat scene that both MacDonald and Lewis make note of. The scene is a memory of Wordsworth as a young boy, stealing a boat on the banks of the lake, Ullswater. As he rows out into the dark lake, he sees a darker mountain rise up off the stern. The vision causes him to feel the moral wrongness of his act and he returns the boat and thinks of this (ll. 81-129). The scene, according to both MacDonald and Lewis, is significant because God in this scene is no pantheistic God who is a sum total of all beings. This is a moral God whom Wordsworth senses is a God that cares about right and wrong, including the theft of small boats. Wordsworth has still been influenced by discussions with Coleridge though while at Goslar they've been separated. Coleridge at this point has moved from his own early pantheism, perhaps under the influence of Kant. Whatever flirtation Wordsworth had with pantheism before February of 1799, by May of 1799 that flirtation is over. The stolen boat scene makes its way into both the 1805 and the 1850 versions of *The Prelude*. If there is any doubt of this, looking at another scene from the 1799 Two-Part *Prelude* should leave us in no doubt. In the "spots of time" portion of the poem, Wordsworth recounts at age thirteen waiting on a wind-blasted hillside near Hawkshead among some sheep, for sight of horses sent by his father to take him and his brothers home. The moment is powerful for him because the horses do not arrive. Instead, he and his brothers get word that their father is dead and they are orphans. He reflects:

> That day so lately passed, when from the crag
> I looked in such anxiety of hope,
> With trite reflections of morality,
> Yet with deepest passion, I bowed low
> To God who thus corrected my desires. (ll. 356-360)

This passage leaves no doubt; this is no pantheistic god, but God, who accepts submission, who is a moral touchstone, who judges desires, and who corrects desires. And this is written by May of 1799. After his brief flirtation with pantheism, what Wordsworth does become and does remain is a panentheist. He finds God visible in nature. He does not confuse God with nature. And his concern for the moral dimension of life is the apparent demise of his short-lived pantheism. For how is a universe in which we all together are god in any way a moral universe? In fact, evidence shows that his transition to Christianity happened earlier than is commonly believed.

Wordsworth's Christianity: "Romantic Anglicanism"

There is an ongoing debate on Wordsworth's early religious convictions, mainly due to the fact that he rarely spoke of them. Still, considering how close in other respects to Wordsworth Lewis is, the subject does bear some consideration here. The debate has included Wordsworth scholars like M.H. Abrams and Jonathan Wordsworth, who have been the most notable proponents for the widely accepted view, that Wordsworth in his younger years was a humanist and verged on the edge of, if not dived deeply into pantheism. Edith Batho, in *The Later Wordsworth*, argued for the view that Wordsworth was a Christian at least in some sense earlier. The most conclusive analysis is the 2001 book by William Ulmer of the University of Alabama, *The Christian Wordsworth: 1798-1805*. Ulmer argues persuasively for a Christian but heterodox Wordsworth as early as 1798. Ulmer marshals considerable textual and biographical evidence that Wordsworth in his early years has a "persistent belief in God" and a "submerged Anglicanism." He writes:

> . . . . Wordsworth's religious development from 1798-1805 was itself essentially continuous, an unbroken process of amplification in which latent Christian "sympathies" became overt Christian "commitments." Wordsworth began either as a theist ready to admire Christianity from afar or, more probably, as an indifferent Christian with Anglican loyalties he found dormant but intact when prodded by Coleridge's inquiries. Faith having its different moods, the distinction between these positions need not have been absolute. (25)

Ulmer is careful to point out that Wordsworth's Christianity was of a revisionist nature and that he was aware of the Higher Criticism going on in Europe at the time. Thus Wordsworth is sometimes critical of the Evangelical theology of his time, uncomfortable with the atonement and much of the Calvinistic emphasis on humanity's sinfulness. Moreover, the influence of Coleridge is tremendous.

> Even if [Wordsworth] quickly learned to dodge issues of dogma in conversations with his new friend, Coleridge by his mere presence offered a standing challenge to Wordsworth to explore and define his own religious convictions. The challenge proved all the less avoidable because poetic interests and motifs borrowed from Coleridge—the idea of the One Life above all—trailed highly specific theological implications in their wake. Wordsworth's response to that challenge thrust him increasingly toward the conventional and conservative while leaving revisionism in its place. He ended, in 1804-1805, with a Romantic Anglicanism which

married Christian tradition to his faith in the human mind as a spiritual power and his confidence in the spiritual joy available in nature. (26)

Ulmer's further analysis is both exhaustive and decisive, and I won't try to summarize more than the main points here that I have already mentioned. The question becomes moot after 1805, the year of the death of the poet's brother, John Wordsworth. This event all scholars recognize as a watershed that moved Wordsworth closer to Anglican orthodoxy and is indisputably Christian.

What is more to the point for this study is how Wordsworth was perceived by those who followed him in the nineteenth century, principally George MacDonald. It will clarify matters to discuss Ulmer's conclusions as they may relate to MacDonald and ultimately Lewis. However, I would go one step further than Ulmer and argue that Wordsworth does actually make something close to a creedal statement. In a letter dated 28 May 1825 to Sir George Beaumont, Wordsworth describes his faith as follows:

> I never had a higher relish for the beauties of Nature than during this spring, nor enjoyed myself more. What manifold reason, my dear Sir George, have you and I to be thankful to Providence! Theologians may puzzle their heads about dogmas as they will; the Religion of gratitude cannot mislead us. Of that we are sure; and Gratitude is the handmaid of Hope, and hope the harbinger of Faith. I look upon Nature, I think of the best part of our species, I lean upon my Friends, and I meditate upon the scriptures, especially the Gospel of St John; and my creed rises up of itself with the ease of an exhalation, yet a Fabric of adamant. (Hill 1984, 228)

This sounds tremendously like a creed. Wordsworth calls it "my creed," and we should probably take his word for it. Moreover, this letter is dated later than or around the date of the Ecclesiastical Sonnets, a time when Wordsworth's orthodoxy is beyond dispute. If we downplay the meditation on scriptures, no doubt it is the creed of the early Wordsworth as well. There are several reasons why this is so: Wordsworth is not, like Coleridge, a systematiser and thinker. He avoids issues of dogma. His faith is empirical and drawn from his contact with nature and scripture. He does not attempt to make it rationally make sense or cover all rational objections. Rather, looking at the changes he made to the 1850 *Prelude* and the occasional statements he makes to Henry Crabb Robinson, it is evident that Wordsworth's faith was pretty much no more nor less than his "Religion of Gratitude" as laid out above, embracing the hopeful concepts of Christianity as part of the mix. In time, meditation on St John's gospel (one of the more soaring and mystic gospels, the least likely to discuss the judgement of God and the most likely to discuss the love of God) and other scripture may have become more important in his creed.

But the remark above about dispensing with theologians and dogma is very telling. Though he came to accept more orthodox dogmas late in life, he never felt himself qualified to understand theology in any academic sense. In an 1840 letter to Henry Alford, he writes,

> For my own part, I have been averse to frequent mention of the mysteries of Christian faith, not from want of a due sense of their momentous nature; but the contrary. I felt it far too deeply to venture on handling the subject as familiarly as many scruple not to do. I am far from blaming them, but let them not blame me, nor turn from my companionship on that account. Besides general reasons of diffidence in treating subjects of holy writ I have some especial ones. I might err in points of faith; and I should not deem my mistakes less to be deprecated because they were expressed in metre. (De Selincourt, *Later Years* 1967, 4. 23-24)

Certainly he felt the Church of England was an institution that needed defending and he abhorred "Romanism." Yet he did not think deeply into the theology of the matter. In addition, his belief in childlike simplicity being closer to Heaven disinclined him to seeking to become more theologically sophisticated. It would have seemed counter-productive to him, for after all, the child is Nature's priest, not the theologian.

But however heterodox and revisionist Wordsworth's Christianity may have been, to the Victorian mind, Wordsworth stood as a poet of faith. Wordsworth's *The Excursion* was widely read as a poem of faith and taken as such. Wordsworth was admired by the leaders of the Oxford Movement and lauded at Oxford with an honorary doctorate, awarded by John Keble, and followed the next day by breakfast with Keble, Frederick Faber and John Henry Newman. Anti-slavery campaigner Thomas Pringle wrote a sonnet in which he referred to Wordsworth as England's Samuel, chosen by God as a sort of prophet (Gill 1998, 240). William Hale White, better known as Mark Rutherford, was raised in a Calvinism which he rejected, but found a road back to faith in reading the poetry of Wordsworth (Gill, 1998, 51-5). This latter account is most telling because in it there is a repeating pattern which we will see in both George MacDonald and to a lesser extent, C.S. Lewis, the moving away from the dogmatic and condemning God, to an immanent God of love that is revealed in the beauty of nature. Most important here is the fact that through all this process of his work being grasped in a specifically Christian context and Wordsworth's being publicly held up as England's Samuel, Wordsworth never protested or demurred. He accepted this role, a role analogous to the role C.S. Lewis played in England during and after the Second World War. And if faith and fear are opposites, many people, like Hale, and MacDonald himself, have made the leap to faith only by rejecting the popular caricature of a Calvinistic concept of a wrathful God. This was what Wordsworth offered that the Victorians embraced, the God of love who is revealed in the beauties of nature, and this without sectarian demands or really much dogma. Gill in his *Wordsworth and the Victorians*, observes that,

> Spiritual power is an almost infinitely elastic term and what people found in, or constructed from Wordsworth, differed greatly. Quakers thought him a Quaker. Anglo-Catholics hailed him as one of themselves. For others it was precisely because it resisted all sectarian labelling that Wordsworth's poetry was so nutritious. (40)

And though Lewis was more attuned to dogma than Wordsworth, much the same could be said of the response to Lewis's work in the twentieth century. Lewis is hailed and embraced by groups as divergent as Latter-Day Saints and Roman Catholics, as well as Baptists and Quakers. Again, as with Wordsworth, the appeal is not so much to a given theological position, because beyond a simple central orthodoxy Lewis labels with the borrowed term, "mere Christianity," Lewis meticulously avoids sectarian positions and focuses, as I will show in later chapters, on the vision of Heaven and the transformation necessary to make one a viable citizen of Heaven. In this, his appeal echoes the appeal of Wordsworth.

There is, however, an aspect of Wordsworth's vision that resonates with MacDonald and Lewis that begins here. First, as has already been mentioned, Lewis observes the human desire to enter into joy:

> We do not merely want to see beauty, though, God knows, even that is bounty enough. We want something else which can hardly be put into words—to be united with the beauty we see, to pass into it, to receive it into ourselves, to bathe in it, to become part of it. (WG 12)

The Prelude as well as "Tintern Abbey" is steeped in this intense desire to embrace the mystery of joy. It is arguably the chief quality of Wordsworth's poetry. Wordsworth as the "Poet of Nature" is attractive to readers in the Nineteenth Century and beyond because he moves away from a stern Calvinistic understanding of faith and life and embraces joy and beauty at a spiritual level, and without any apparent dogmatism or sectarianism. MacDonald will take this lightening of Christianity and develop it into a sense of what I call divine paradox, which will influence both Lewis and Chesterton.

Coleridge and the Imagination

One objection to my contention of Lewis's Romanticism is his own disavowal in print of it. The specifics are as follows: George Sayer in his biography of Lewis both maintains that Lewis never made much sense of Coleridge's distinction between the fancy and the imagination, and alternately that Lewis feared the Romanticism of his early youth that led to out of control sensuality, as represented in the country south of the main road in *The Pilgrim's Regress*. Sayer is right as far as he goes, but this distinction Lewis is making between imagination which might lead to a realization of eternal truths and imagination that leads to what Lewis called "Christina dreams," that is, ego fantasizing, is one possible way of looking at what Coleridge meant by the distinction between fancy and the imagination. Coleridge's "fancy" might easily be Lewis's "Christina dreams" (Sayer 1988, 82, 123). As subsequent chapters will show, Lewis disdains that which might be called Romantic either because it involves a surrender to the illusions of sensuality, as is symbolized in the country south of the road in *The Pilgrim's Regress*, or because that Romanticism assumes a level of intrinsic human virtue that does not exist. Actually, the two concepts are closely related, though separate. The second objection is answered in MacDonald's concept of the sanctification of Romanticism in the Christian faith. The first is answered in Lewis's rejection of what Coleridge calls the "fancy" as explained above.

Coleridge's Platonism

Lewis shares with Coleridge a Platonic world view in terms strikingly similar. Lewis mentions Coleridge more than twenty times in print. The two most notable references are first, faulting Coleridge through the reverse logic of Screwtape for advocating overly emotional and vague prayer (SL 25). The second and more significant recorded mention of Coleridge is fittingly in the opening of *The Abolition of Man* (AM 14). He cites a story of Coleridge at a waterfall in Scotland on his 1803 tour with Wordsworth and Wordsworth's sister, Dorothy. This story can alternately be found in Dorothy Wordsworth's journal of the trip (Dorothy Wordsworth 1997, 63-4). The incident is mentioned in passing because Coleridge is pleased when one tourist calls the waterfall "sublime"—a term that Coleridge took to mean having transcendental qualities that spoke of another existence beyond our own—and the tourist's wife calls the waterfall "pretty," which galled Coleridge. "Gaius and Titius" blunder into Lewis's cross hairs by commenting that the word sublime here is a statement about Coleridge's feelings as he looks at the waterfall, a thoroughly subjectivist interpretation. Lewis then proceeds to dismember this subjectivism for the remainder of the book. Any other mention of Coleridge is swept away. However, though it passes quickly here, Coleridge is champion of an intrinsic sublime, a transcendental and objective phenomenon, and given Lewis's avowed Platonism, also it is a platonic sublime that holds significance beyond the boundaries of this world. Indeed, in another place, Coleridge makes a distinction that has tremendous echoes in Lewis's own arguments against the materialistic worldview of "Scientism."

> The difference between Aristotle and Plato is that which will remain as long as we are men and there is any difference between man and man in point of opinion. Plato, with Pythagoras before him, had conceived that the phenomenon or outward appearance, all that we call thing or matter, is but as it were a language by which the invisible (that which is not the object of our senses) communicates its existence to our finite beings . . Aristotle, on the contrary, affirmed that all our knowledge had begun in experience, had begun through the senses, and that from the senses only we could take our notions of reality . . . It was the first way in which, plainly and distinctly, two opposite systems were placed before the mind of the world. (Coleridge 1949, 186-8)

This is the argument that Lewis uses in his essay "Meditation in a Toolshed," that the mere looking *at* things is not sufficient for knowing them, a basic tenet of a materialistic world-view that holds that only empirical science can be used to discern truth. Lewis, admittedly a Platonist, clearly stands on the platonic side of Coleridge's divide and spends a large portion of his written output defending the platonic side. One hears old Professor Kirke lamenting in *The Last Battle*, "It's all in Plato, all in Plato: bless me, what *do* they teach them at these schools!"(LB 161)

Reilly in his 1971 study details the long and deep effect of Coleridge's thought on Owen Barfield, but a study of Barfield's own writings on Lewis does not indicate any possibility of a secondary influence of Coleridge on Lewis via Barfield. Reilly's contention that Lewis got from Coleridge the two Kantian categories of the "Practical" and "Speculative Intellect" is likewise a long reach (140). It is more likely that Lewis in reading Coleridge found a kindred spirit in the matter of Platonism to which his mind had already formed. If we can trace any clear influence on Lewis from Wordsworth or Coleridge, it most likely takes the form of indirect influence through the good offices of George MacDonald.

CHAPTER THREE

MacDonald, Chesterton, and Barfield

If we find that Lewis does not readily acknowledge Wordsworth's influence, it is perhaps because that influence was initially mediated through George MacDonald. That is, if Lewis could not embrace Wordsworth's Romanticism undiluted, he was able to embrace completely the Romanticism of George MacDonald. Certainly Lewis read Wordsworth for himself, and we will document his complex response in a later chapter. But MacDonald's version of Wordsworth's thought, or perhaps it might be more accurate to say, MacDonald's vision, developed from his own faith and elements of Wordsworth's vision, a whole new creation, was very palatable to Lewis.

Wordsworth's influence on George MacDonald has already been well documented, especially by critic Roderick McGillis. McGillis' article "Childhood and Growth: George MacDonald and William Wordsworth," details a series of steps of spiritual development that a person might go through to attain a pure spiritual childhood, which for MacDonald, is not something to be left behind but to be attained. McGillis's wide reading and understanding of MacDonald is impressive and his exegesis of MacDonald's categories and the sequence in which they occur is convincing. However, it does present a critical problem, as he repeatedly must admit that even in these stages, Wordsworth understands them differently, ie, for Wordsworth childhood has an end and for MacDonald it is a spiritual state to be attained. All this raises a larger question of what we mean by influence, an area in which it is wise to practice a little critical caution. Doubtless MacDonald's considerable and acknowledged influence on Lewis is well-documented (GMD xxxii). When we talk of Lewis being influenced, we are actually talking about at least two processes. The first might be the kind of influence where a latter author imitates a structure employed by an earlier author they have read. For example, clearly Lewis borrows the idea of children having adventures from the Edith Nesbitt stories. The second might be the more subtle, and therefore difficult to prove, worldview or at least partial worldview adopted by one writer after reading the work of an earlier writer. We might say that the latter writer gained a taste for the flavor in the work of the earlier writing and that flavor emerges in the work of the latter writer. Without actual acknowledgment from the latter writer that such was their intent, we are arguing inductively at best and working towards what at most can be considered a plausible assumption.

Such is the case in our study. There is a tremendous amount of textual evidence pointing toward the conclusion that Lewis through MacDonald got certain central ideas and a sense of vision. And if Lewis enjoys Wordsworth, especially *The Prelude,* it is because in it he recognized elements in MacDonald which had so moved and influenced him. McGillis's close and carefully reasoned analysis has considerable merit, but I very much doubt that Lewis either consciously or subconsciously intended anything so complex in his writing. Though McGillis isolates some seven concepts that McDonald may have drawn from Wordsworth, I believe there are essentially three concepts, or perhaps 'flavors' that Lewis finds in MacDonald that he later finds attractive in his re-readings of Wordsworth's *Prelude.* These are: the Romantic concept of the child and the spiritual élan of childhood; the viewing of nature as a kind of transmitter of the Divine Presence and therefore, by definition, a kind of sacrament; the sense, transmitted through the beauty of nature, of a loving God who is the source and author of beauty, and that being drawn to this is to be drawn into the deeper spiritual realm. This third 'flavor' stands in contrast to the more Calvinist emphasis on doctrine, dogma and human sinfulness. As I have shown in the previous chapter, Wordsworth displayed a serious antipathy to the Calvinist model in Christian faith, to the point of heterodoxy, if William Ulmer is correct. Rejecting the stern religion of his earlier years, MacDonald , eventually found a way to merge the vision of Romanticism with the Christian faith, even to the point of skirting the edges of universalism. What for Wordsworth was a move away from the thought of the Eighteenth Century, and thus a revolution for him, for MacDonald becomes much more. For Wordsworth, this bright vision of the divine, proceeding from visible and sensible nature is the surprising revolution in faith. Macdonald grasps this and takes it further. With Wordsworth's sense of the attraction to light and joy as opposed to darkness and condemnation, and a New Testament sense of paradox, MacDonald, throughout his writing career creates this sense of what I have called Divine Paradox. Thus the first shall be last, he who would save his life must lose it, and freedom is achieved through obedience. These and other biblical paradoxes permeate all of MacDonald's novels and fantasies, matched with Romantic imagery of light and dark. Thus MacDonald's character, the princess Irene, is able to rescue and bring to freedom the miner boy, Curdie, from the goblins by following a thread into the mine and out, which symbolizes obedience. It is these Divine Paradoxes which become the hallmark of G.K. Chesterton's writing later and also, though less frequently than Chesterton, a common feature of C.S. Lewis's writing.

Lewis exhibits far more caution than MacDonald, as we saw in the first chapter of this study that Lewis is very careful to part ways with the sort of pantheism that Wordsworth seems to stand for. Though, however much Lewis is careful to stay within bounds of orthodoxy, for him, as for MacDonald and Wordsworth, the draw to faith comes primarily through the imagination and the heart.

The connections, or perhaps the similarities of the 'preferred flavors,' will become apparent if we look into MacDonald's essay on Wordsworth from *A Dish of Orts*. MacDonald's essay, titled, "Wordsworth's Poetry," makes a rather bold assertion from the start. "The very element in which the mind of Wordsworth lived and moved was a Christian pantheism." (MacDonald, *Orts* 1893, 245) MacDonald will explain this but it is notable here that he is coming up with his own solution regarding the suitability of Wordsworth's Christianity. Though Lewis would choke on the combination of "Christian" and "pantheism," MacDonald does not. His solution to the paradox is very much in line with William Ulmer's thought, that Christian as a term may be applied to trends of thought that bear elements of Christian ideas without having to meet a complete litmus test of orthodoxy. MacDonald explains his extraordinary statement by defining pantheism in a way that is only marginally pantheistic.

> This world is not merely a thing which God hath made, subjecting it to laws; but it is an expression of the thought, the feeling, the heart of God himself. And so it must be; because, if man be the child of God, would he not feel to be out of his element if he lived in a world which came, not from the heart of God, but only from his hand? This Christian pantheism, this belief that God is in everything, and showing himself in everything, has been much brought t the light by the poets of the past generation, and has its influence still, I hope, upon the poets of the present. (MacDonald, *Orts* 1893, 246)

Thus what MacDonald means by pantheism is not the standard definition that all living things together are God, a position to which Lewis absolutely objected. For MacDonald, the world is a work of art, loved into being by God, signed by the artist. Humanity is happy in the beauty of nature because it is the Divine permeating down into our ordinary existence. For MacDonald nature operates as a sacrament. The world is not God, and MacDonald cites the stolen boat passage in Wordsworth's

The Prelude (Bk 1, lines 357-400) to demonstrate that Wordsworth distinguishes between nature and the moral God who created her. MacDonald goes on to lay out three ways that Wordsworth learned from nature, to which he was so sensitive. The first two, amusement and mere moral lessons, MacDonald passes over rather quickly. The third he is clearly more interested in.

> There is yet a higher and more sustained influence exercised by nature, and that takes effect when she puts a man into that mood or condition in which thoughts come of themselves. That is perhaps the best thing that can be done for us, the best at least that nature can do. It is certainly higher than mere intellectual teaching. That nature did this for Wordsworth is very clear; and it is easily intelligible. If the world proceeded from the imagination of God, it is easy to believe that that which proceeded from the imagination of God should rouse the best thoughts in the mind of a being who proceeded from the love of God. This I think is the relation between man and the world (MacDonald, *Orts* 1893, 254).

MacDonald concludes with the thought, "When we understand the Word of God, then we understand the works of God; when we know the nature of the artist, we know his pictures" (256). Throughout the rest of the essay he analyzes Wordsworth's attitude toward science, which MacDonald endorses, and discusses Wordsworth's use of common diction. But the heart of what MacDonald draws from Wordsworth is this theology of nature, this "pantheism" as MacDonald defines it. This point has several vital implications: first, the vital importance of imagination, an indisputable Romantic principal, in this case, the imagination of God. God creates through imagination, and therefore imagination is a god-like power, and to use the imagination is to use that within our humanity that was granted us when God made Adam and Eve in his image. Second, because humanity is the product of the imagination of God, the beauty of nature, proceeding from the imagination of God is that which is calculated to "rouse the best thoughts in the mind of a being who proceeded from the love of God." We are hard-wired to find God in the beauty of nature.

Third, though it may be difficult to prove that Wordsworth thought the things that MacDonald is imputing to him here, I would speculate that at very least, the later Wordsworth would not object to them, though he would demur from trying to articulate his vision in the manner that MacDonald has here. And even if this is not what Wordsworth meant when he wrote the poetry that MacDonald cites in the article, Lewis, following MacDonald a century later shows definite signs of reading Wordsworth in the light of MacDonald's reading of Wordsworth.

But perhaps the most vital element here that Lewis will pick up is the sense in Wordsworth, seized upon here by MacDonald, of the intentionality of human existence. MacDonald does not focus on it, although by the publication date of 1893, the whole post-Darwinian era of Naturalism was in full swing. But in MacDonald's account of Wordsworth's thought, humanity is the product of the Divine imagination as much as a great painting is the product of the imagination of a great painter. Indeed, Wordsworth is absolutely certain of the rightness of everything. In the final stanza of "Tintern Abbey" he writes to his sister:

> Knowing that Nature never did betray
> The heart that loved her; 'tis her privilege
> Through all the years of this our life, to lead
> From joy to joy: for she can so inform
> The mind that is within us, so impress
> With quietness and beauty, and so feed
> With lofty thoughts, that neither evil tongues,
> Rash judgments, nor the sneers of selfish men
> Nor greetings where no kindness is, nor all
> The dreary intercourse of daily life,
> Shall ever prevail against us, or disturb
> Our cheerful faith, that all which we behold
> Is full of blessings. (ll. 122-134)

For MacDonald this seems so self-evident that he almost fails to comment on it. But the world in 1893 was far from convinced that existence was eminently meaningful.

C.S. Lewis, writing almost a century later in the shadow of two world wars and philosophical movements such as Modernism and Existentialism, each with heavy undertones of Nihilism, is fighting on a different front. Lewis himself as a young atheist felt that his position was self-evident primarily because the world is meaningless. He begins the book, *The Problem of Pain*, by summarizing the reasons he was once an atheist, and they amount to Nihilism (PP 13-15). Once Lewis switches polarities and becomes a defender of Christianity, he is in constant combat with the nihilistic worldview. In his fiction, as we will see in later chapter, the fictional settings are imbued with this sense, this 'flavor' rising up through Wordsworth and MacDonald, that the world is eminently meaningful, a product of the imagination and willed creation of God and no accident. In Narnia Aslan sings the world into being from his thought. The children visit when Aslan wills it and even when Jill tells Aslan that they asked to come into Narnia, Aslan replies that, "You would not have called to me unless I had been calling to you" (SC 19). Lewis's works are all pervaded with this theme of the pursuing God, which is found also in MacDonald, that there are no accidents, and that humanity is loved into being by the imagination of God and that every event, no matter how perplexing or ugly they may seem to us, is within the plan of God for each individual human.

Secondly, and as a corollary to the first concept, this meaning-imbued universe is not only given purpose and direction by its Creator, but is subject to a definite moral code. Wordsworth makes this quite clear in the stolen boat episode of *The Prelude*, which MacDonald is careful to quote. Lewis takes both these positions not only as central to his imagery in his fantasy and science fiction, but as his apologetic stance as well.

Perhaps the work of MacDonald that most shows the influence of Wordsworth is *Sir Gibbie*. *Sir Gibbie* is essentially a Wordsworthian vision set in MacDonald's Scotland. Gibbie is the innocent child in the industrially evil city of Aberdeen. A brutal murder sends him flying west along the River Dee till he makes his way to a humble shepherd's cottage high on a lonely mountain that could just as easily be a fell in Wordsworth's Lake District. The shepherd people are innocent, wise and good, as in Wordsworth. And though the ending is happier than some Wordsworthian tales, the final joy is reached only through pain and destruction of a severe flood and the downfall of the great from their heights.

In the end, MacDonald sees a divine hand in nature, and believes that Wordsworth does as well. This mystic and sacramental view is echoed in Lewis. David Downing points out that MacDonald believed in nature being a kind of sacrament by the Anglican definition and even quotes MacDonald calling it that in the mouth of a character in *The Portent* (Downing 2005, 44). Downing relates this to Lewis's own mystical understanding of nature. He quotes George Sayer in his biography of Lewis. "Jack's [Lewis's] view of nature was essentially mystical. He often saw in it 'the signature of all things.'" (Sayer 1988, 148).

Tying together these three threads of the spiritual élan of the child, seeing nature as a sacrament, and being drawn by beauty rather than coerced by guilt, George MacDonald created a redeemed Romanticism that answers Coleridge's question of the dark side of Romanticism, by sanctifying it on Christ's cross. For MacDonald Romantic longing is longing after Christ's Heaven, as Mossy and Tangle discover in "The Golden Key." Yet Mossy and Tangle both have to die to become fully alive, and so the burden of dark human nature is healed in Christ's sacrifice and our death to the old life and rebirth as new men and women. These ideas find their root in Wordsworth and their branching out in

Lewis. Perhaps Henry Crabb Robinson left his bequest to MacDonald in appreciation of this sanctifying of Romanticism.

Aside from MacDonald, perhaps the greatest influence on Lewis's later writing and thought is G.K. Chesterton. There is little connection between Chesterton and Wordsworth. Chesterton wrote a short essay on Wordsworth as a newspaper column dated December 30, 1933, and titled "Wordsworth, Early and Late." The piece contemplates whether it is fair to overvalue Wordsworth's youthful years at the expense of his later years, or whether all his opinions can be traced to his experience of the French Revolution. Unlike MacDonald, Chesterton isn't much interested in Wordsworth's world view if this article is any indication. He seems more interested in the correct history of Wordsworth's politics (Chesterton, *Collected* . . . 396-400). Nevertheless, Chesterton's own view is unashamedly Romantic. Like Lewis after him, Chesterton's apologetic and other essays are a fine mix of image and analogy with dialectic and all couched in paradox. Indeed, it is hard for Chesterton to write two sentences without using a surprising paradox. Perhaps the most indicative work of Chesterton is his 1908 book, *Orthodoxy*. The subtitle is *The Romance of Faith*. Romance as such is a broadly defined word, but close examination of the text shows that by it, Chesterton means that the grasp of faith by the imagination is the most reasonable thing a man can do. Starting with the introduction, Chesterton explains why he is writing this book and that he will not be trying to writing a purely deductive argument. "I have attempted in a vague and personal way, in a set of mental pictures rather than a series of deductions, to state the philosophy in which I have come to believe" (9). From the first and by his own admission, Chesterton is arguing from the imagination in good Romantic tradition.

He follows this with one of his most striking images, the story of a man who left England to discover and explore a South Sea island, and in his confusion landed at Brighton and began to explore his home with new eyes. Chesterton uses this paradox as a controlling metaphor for the rest of the volume, but from the first page, he is invoking a Divine Paradox, in the tradition of MacDonald. Chesterton had a great reverence for MacDonald and wrote the preface to Greville MacDonald's biography of his father in which Chesterton praised George MacDonald as "the morning star of the reunion." Chesterton writes of MacDonald's *The Princess and the Goblin*:

> But in a certain rather special sense I for one can really testify to a book that has made a difference to my whole existence, which helped me to see things in a certain way from the start; a vision of things which even so real a revolution as a change of religious allegiance has substantially only crowned and confirmed. Of all the stories I ever read ... it remains the most

real, the most realistic, in the exact sense of the phrase the most like life. It
is called *The Princess and the Goblin*, and is by George MacDonald....
(Greville McDonald 1924, 9)

Following this opening paradox of the man setting out and discovering
his own home, Chesterton writes of "the rich romantic nature of the hero"
(9) and follows by defining this term.

> . . . the thing I propose to take as common ground between myself and any
> average reader, is this desirability of and active and imaginative life,
> picturesque and full of poetical curiosity, a life such as western man at any
> rate always seems to have denied. (10)

Further on in the same chapter, Chesterton launches into a long
discussion on madness and reason. He insists that poets are the sanest of
people (16-17). In an argument that echoes Shelley's *Defence of Poetry*,
Chesterton writes that, "Imagination does not breed insanity. Exactly what
does breed insanity is reason" (17). By this he means excessive and
obsessive reason, and he follows with numerous examples.

In later chapters, Chesterton argues for a child-like appreciation of life
and of literature, defending fairy stories in a way that Tolkien and Lewis
were later to echo. He writes,

> My first and last philosophy, . . . I learnt in the nursery. The things I
> believed most then, the things I believe most now, are the things called
> fairy tales. They seem to me to be the entirely reasonable things. They are
> not fantasies: compared with them other things are fantastic. Compared
> with them religion and rationalism are both abnormal, though religion is
> abnormally right and rationalism abnormally wrong. Fairyland is nothing
> but the sunny country of common sense. (49)

For Chesterton, in good Romantic fashion, reason must be balanced
with common sense, which is perceived through the imagination. This will
be echoed in Lewis later on. Chesterton is close to a definition of the right
relationship of reason to imagination. Yet, MacDonald did not clearly
answer the question of the place of reason within the whole.

Arguably the greatest achievement of Lewis was to reconcile this
perennial division between reason and Romanticism, between reason and
imagination. The reference occurs in Lewis's essay "Bluspels and
Flalansferes: A Semantic Nightmare," which appears in *Selected Literary
Essays*. The essay itself is an explanation of the growth of language
through metaphor, essentially a affirmation of all that Barfield argues in

his book *Poetic Diction*, which Lewis admits was "important" to him. (SBJ 200) Lewis in the conclusion of the essay writes:

> But it must not be supposed that I am in any sense putting forward the imagination as the organ of truth. We are not talking of truth, but of meaning: meaning which is the antecedent condition both of truth and falsehood, whose antithesis is not error but nonsense. I am a rationalist. For me, reason is the natural organ of truth; but imagination is the organ of meaning. Imagination, producing new metaphors or revivifying old, is not the cause of truth, but its condition. It is, I confess, undeniable that such a view indirectly implies a kind of truth or rightness in the imagination itself. (SLE 265)

Jane Hipolito has argued that *Poetic Diction* is the significant point of agreement between these two friends who did not agree on everything (Hipolito 2007, 228).   Barfield's *Poetic Diction* expands greatly and originally on the idea of Wordsworth and Coleridge that we "half-create" reality in perceiving it. Barfield argues that this is due to the fact that all language is fossilized metaphor and built up by accretions of metaphor over the centuries. This far, Lewis follows and agrees with Barfield. Hipolito points out that Lewis spent significant time and energy critiquing the early drafts of *Poetic Diction*, and Barfield dedicated the book to him. In a letter of 27 May 1928, Lewis congratulates Barfield on the publication of the book saying:

> I think in general that I am going to agree with the whole book more than we thought I did. We really are at one about imagination as the source of meanings, i.e. almost of *objects*. We both agree that it is the *prius* of truth. (CLCSL1 762)

Of course, Barfield and Lewis disagree on Barfield's concept of human consciousness evolving, and the idea of the imagination. Barfield writes in his essay "Lewis and Historicism" in *Owen Barfield on C.S. Lewis*, that Lewis was incapable of thinking of humanity as a concept except perhaps as a way to describe the sum total of human beings. Thus Barfield argues that Lewis was incapable of Historicism, meaning that Lewis was incapable of conceiving of history as a picture of humanity evolving into a higher spiritual plane as Barfield did. For Lewis, this would be another form of Evolutionism, and not credible. What is more significant is how much Lewis and Barfield agree on this central understanding of metaphor and imagination as spelled out in *Poetic Diction.*

His statement from "Bluspels and Flalanspheres" is Lewis's most plain statement of the relation of reason to imagination, even if it does not constitute a theory of imagination that satisfies his friend, Barfield. Neither does Lewis have any sort of original "theory of reason." As a student of Kirkpatrick, logic for Lewis is the groundwork of existence, and the truthful measure of all else. On the other side, for Lewis, the imagination is the use and production of metaphor. It is pictures in the mind that accompany words, that therefore become the condition by which meaning is conveyed and reality perceived, as in *Poetic Diction*. Nor does Lewis have any patience with the suppositions that came with Poststructuralism. Words convey realities that exist beyond the grasp of the minds. Words do not create these realities, nor are they one thing for one person and another for another person. They are not subjective. They convey truth, concrete and verifiable, which in a platonic sense, exists behind our mental pictures conveyed in words. Barfield goes beyond this in what is probably some of the most significant and under-appreciated philosophy of the twentieth century in his subsequent books. Reilly's chapters on the subject are thorough and eye-opening. It is hoped that Barfield might yet come to be as fully appreciated as he deserves in the history of philosophy and historical linguistics. But our study is focused on Lewis.

More important to Lewis's place as a seminal though dissident thinker in the twentieth century, reason is the "organ of truth." To divorce oneself from reason as much twentieth century thought does, is to descend into nonsense and madness. But to leave all to reason, to divorce oneself from the imagination, is to lose meaning. Both are necessary. For Lewis, as a Christian, both are metaphorically speaking, languages by which the Creator communicates to His creatures. They are not contradictory but rather mutually correcting of each the other's limitations. Lewis has found a concrete and viable way to reconcile reason and imagination in human thought in the twentieth century.

Thus, Lewis, recognizing the importance of imagination as the organ of meaning, in his fiction and even his metaphor-rich apologetics, conveys like MacDonald and Wordsworth before him, a meaningful cosmos, in which God has imagined us into being and has clothed us like the lilies of the field and witnessed the fall of every sparrow, calculating them in the Divine Plan for the cosmos. Lewis is entirely counter-nihilistic, in a cosmos where reason and imagination are in balance and the Divine is a thin membrane away from the mundane world.

CHAPTER FOUR

THE PRELUDE, WORDSWORTH AND LEWIS

Lewis's Reaction to *The Prelude*

Of the books that Lewis listed as most influential in his interview in the June 6, 1962 issue of *The Christian Century*, only two are books of English poetry. The first is George Herbert's *The Temple*, and the second is William Wordsworth's *The Prelude*. By influential here Lewis means those pieces of literature which have most shaped his heart and mind. After all, the list was produced for a popular American church magazine and Lewis, who was always intensely aware of his audience, would not have given such a publication a scholarly list. In fact, it is rather doubtful that Lewis ever analyzed who most influenced his writing style. The question would have had no interest for him.

In a letter to Arthur Greeves of 18 September 1919 Lewis records first reading *the Prelude*. He finds it "funn[y]" that he actually likes it, and feels it is a poem best read "while smoking a pipe" (CLCSL1 466). He admits to preferring the first book. In a subsequent letter dated 18 October 1919, he writes, "I finished the Prelude and like it. It is about as bad as a poem could be in some ways but one considers the great passages not too dearly bought at the price of the rest" (CLCSL1 468). By the time the mature Lewis admits that he regularly re-reads *The Prelude* in 1962, I think we my conjecture that his taste for the work has deepened and his judgment of it has grown less flippant. Indeed, re-reading a poem over a forty-three year period indicates a deep devotion to a work. So we can assume by his own account that *The Prelude* deeply moved Lewis. This would be the 1850 version, rewritten between 1832 and 1838, the "Christian" *Prelude*, if you will. The existence of the 1805 version was known in Lewis's lifetime—as of 1926--and as widely read as Lewis was, he may well have read it. But we have no written comments by him on it, so its difference did not apparently affect him. We can also assume that he reread it frequently, as we know that he was a frequent re-reader. We also have his 23 April 1951 letter to Dom Bede Griffiths, OSB, in which he apologizes for not reading Lubac because he has been reading *The Prelude* while ill and on holiday. He writes, "it and the *Aeneid* . . . are the two long poems to wh. I most often return" (CLCSL3 111). In defining the numinous in *The Problem of Pain*, Lewis cites the stolen boat episode from Book I of *The Prelude* (lines 357-400), saying,

> Going back about a century we find copious examples [of the numinous] in Wordsworth—perhaps the finest being that passage in the first book of the *Prelude* where he describes his experience while rowing on the lake in the stolen boat. (PP 18)

It also seems that whatever else of Wordsworth Lewis read, (and his use of the title of a Wordsworth sonnet "Surprised by Joy" makes one suspect that he read *all*) *The Prelude* seems to have had a special place for him. Yet, Lewis does not embrace Wordsworth entirely, but is critical of him in a way that makes one wonder why he re-read *The Prelude* so often.

The Primary Element of Vision: Heaven

For Wordsworth "there is a spirit in the wood," and that spirit, found by him in nature, elevates his heart and mind so that by its influence, he believed he became a better person. For Wordsworth, nature and the influence of nature have a morally improving influence, though as he pointed out in his poem "Peter Bell," simple contact with nature is useless without an open human heart that can take in the lessons it teaches. This alone would be significant but unmoving were it not for the sense of grandeur and awe that Wordsworth communicates, that is simply so overwhelming we read some of his work and feel that we are on the borders of Heaven itself, a technique Lewis successfully recreates in the Narnia Chronicles.

So we might say that Wordsworth sensed the spirit in the woods and the heavenly glory in nature; MacDonald affirmed that glory and attributed it to the Christian God. And Lewis refined and finished this Romantic/Christian vision. To MacDonald ought to go the credit for being the father of Christian Romanticism, and to Lewis perhaps the credit for refining and finishing it. Certainly Chesterton, who might be accused of being a Christian Romantic, pays tribute to MacDonald in his foreword to Greville MacDonald's biography of his parents. And certainly, MacDonald is the founder of the tradition of literary fantasy being used as a subtle vehicle for the Christian message, something both Lewis and Tolkien surely enlarged and developed.

Interestingly, in his time, as pointed out in a previous chapter, Wordsworth played something like this role of literary spokesman for faith and virtue. In the later years of his long life, Wordsworth was venerated by the Victorians for the moral value of his literature, a role he never denied or tried to belittle. Rather he accepted it. His long poem, *The Excursion*, the poem most of his contemporaries best knew him by, includes extensive sections of dialogue by a holy pastor counseling a right view of life and its tragedies. In fact it bears much resemblance to similar sort of preachy passages in MacDonald's novels, where the action stops for a character to give us a sermon. The appeal of Wordsworth's presentations of the moral life to the Victorians can only have been helped by their having been couched in appealing poetry that touched the heart, and not just in dull books of virtue for young persons. Yet Wordsworth did not, like MacDonald, Lewis and Tolkien, move in fantasy, only brushing the edges of fantasy in his work. The people and places he knew were so much more intense for him as central images. Wordsworth's faith lies in this present world and at least in his early work, in an optimistic assessment of the goodness of human nature. This is where Lewis faults him.

Nature of the Translation: Lewis's Caveat on Wordsworth

This brings us to the question of how Lewis regarded Wordsworth. What's interesting is that Lewis regularly reread *The Prelude* and took the title of his autobiography from a Wordsworth sonnet, and yet when he does mention Wordsworth, he is critical. This is because though Wordsworth saw intimations of redemption in nature, Lewis knows that both Romanticism and even nature herself need redemption. He warned that both eroticism and occultism lurk on the quest for Romantic longing, or *Sehnsucht* (CR 22). In "The Weight of Glory" Lewis scolds Wordsworth for mistaking moments of romantic longing for the past. "Wordsworth's expedient was to identify it with certain moments in his own past. But this is all a cheat. If Wordsworth had gone back to those moments in the past, he would not have found the thing itself, but only a reminder of it" (WG 7). In *Surprised by Joy* Lewis laments that in his youth he worked hard to find the thing desired in the vicinity of where the desire had stabbed him. Thus a moment of desire in seeing an Arthur Rackham illustration of Norse mythology led Lewis to become an expert in Norse mythology. But as he says, "Finally I woke from building the temple to find that the God had flown." Alluding to the Immortality Ode, he continues, "I was in the Wordsworthian predicament, lamenting that a 'glory' had passed away" (SJ 165-6). He goes on to add, "I insisted that he [God] ought to appear in the temple I had built him; . . . . Wordsworth, I believe, made this mistake all his life. I am sure that all that sense of loss of vanished vision which fills *The Prelude* was itself vision of the same kind, if only he could have believed it" (SJ 167). But Lewis's most extensive argument with Wordsworth is found in his discussion on nature in *The Four Loves*. At first he distinguishes between the love of nature which pays attention to particulars, like that of a botanist, and the love of nature that takes in scenic vistas, or as the nineteenth century would have called them, "prospects." And he agrees with Wordsworth to this degree, but he follows with an important distinction worth quoting at length. He writes:

> While you are busying yourself with this critical and discriminating activity you lose what really matters—the "moods of time and season," the "spirit" of the place. And of course Wordsworth is right. . . . . .
>
> It is the "moods" or the "spirit" that matter. Nature-lovers want to receive as fully as possible whatever nature, at each particular time and place, is, so to speak, saying. . . . They lay themselves bare to the sheer quality of every countryside, every hour of the day. They want to absorb it into themselves, to be coloured through and through by it.
>
> This experience, like so many others, after being lauded to the skies in the nineteenth century, has been debunked by the moderns. And one must certainly concede to the debunkers that Wordsworth, not when he was communicating it as a poet, but when he was merely talking about it as a philosopher (or philophaster), said some very silly things. It is silly, unless you have found any evidence, to believe that flowers enjoy the air they breathe, and sillier not to add that, if this were true, flowers would undoubtedly have pains as well as pleasures. Nor have many people been taught moral philosophy by an "impulse from a vernal wood."
>
> If they were, it would not necessarily be the sort of moral philosophy Wordsworth would have approved. It might be that of ruthless competition. For some moderns I think it is. They love nature in so far as, for them, she calls to "the dark gods in the blood"; not although, but because, sex and hunger and sheer power operate there without pity or shame.
>
> If you take nature as a teacher she will teach you exactly the lessons you had already decided to learn; (FL 34-36)

Lewis has touched on Romanticism's fatal flaw. The Romantics rejected the focus on reason that was characteristic of the Enlightenment which throws one on the imagination and the feelings for guidance on the way of truth and understanding in this world. But the imagination also has a dark side.

Longing Not Enough—No Beauty We Could Desire

Lewis's own poetic expression of the need to pursue something beyond our romantic longings is expressed in what I believe to be his best poem, "No Beauty We Could Desire."

> Not in Nature, not even in Man, but in one
> Particular Man, with a date, so tall, weighing
> So much, talking Aramaic, having learned a trade;
> Not in all food, not in all bread and wine
> (Not, I mean, as my littleness requires)
> But this wine, this bread . . . no beauty we could desire. (CP 138)

This touches on the most commonly cited piece of Lewis's Romanticism, which I have avoided for reasons explained in the introduction: Lewis's lifelong interest in the longing for joy and its transcendental significance. But as Lewis says at the ending of *Surprised by Joy*, joy is but a signpost (238). Lewis would not have us rest in the ecstasy of nature's beauty as Wordsworth would. This is the other part of Lewis's understanding of the relation of reason to imagination. Imagination gives meaning but it is not a road that one can follow. That function is given to reason alone. Lewis would have us move on to the seemingly mundane, a Jewish carpenter from the nowhere province of Galilee, speaking Aramaic, executed by the Romans, and even plainer things like the simple bread and the simple wine. Certainly Wordsworth would agree that there is beauty in simple people and simple things, but Lewis has focused the vision even further than Wordsworth ever publicly dared.

This is what might be called Lewis's Principle of Inattention, a concept Lewis draws from Christ's words that one must lose one's life to save it. In Lewis's thought, imagination gives meaning, but to pursue the metaphors and images is futile. One must turn away to the mundane realities one lives with, and follow the dictates of reason. In thus losing the good the imagination perceives, one finds it in the other direction. *Pilgrim's Regress* is built upon a metaphor that expresses this. Pilgrim John walks toward the beautiful mountains ahead of him, only to find in the end they were the back side of the mountains upon which he was born and raised.

In *Studies on Words* Lewis devotes a chapter to the word "Nature" that is mainly a small treatise on the linguistic history of the word. What is very telling is the last section titled, "'Nature' in Eighteenth and Nineteenth Century Poetry." Lewis summarizes Wordsworth and Coleridge's use of the word 'Nature' as ". . . the country as opposed to the town, though it may in particular passages be extended to cover the sun, moon, and stars" (SW 73). Then, as if in answer to the dismissive tone of this first definition, Lewis goes on to say,

> This does not at all mean that the poets are talking nonsense. They are expressing a way of looking at things which must arise when towns become very large and the urban way of life very different from the rural. When this happens most people (not all) feel a sense of relief and restoration on getting out into the country; it is a serious emotion and a recurrent one, a proper theme for high poetry. Philosophically, no doubt, it is superficial to say we have escaped from the works of man to those of *Nature* when in fact, smoking a man-made pipe and swinging a man-made stick, wearing our man-made boots and clothes, we pause on a man-made bridge to look down on the banked, narrowed, and deepened river which man has made out of the original wide, shallow, and swampy mess, and across it, at a landscape which has only its larger geological features in common with that which would have existed if man had never interfered. But we are expressing something we really feel. (SW 73-4)

This description is delightful if one has read Lewis's biography, because it is precisely a description of Lewis himself on one of his walks, a touch of autobiography slipping into a linguistic study. But the main issue here is the clear statement of balance Lewis holds in his view of Wordsworth's and Coleridge's view of nature. Certainly, Lewis is far away from any sort of wide-eyed pantheism as he has been at pains to make clear all along. Yet, the Romantic poets are "expressing something we really feel." Pantheistic nature worship is misleading, to be sure, but the attention to nature as a conduit of divine grace, if we will only look at it with the side of our eye and not straight on, is a valid thing. The Principle of Inattention is vital if we are to see the "patches of Godlight" (LM 91) in a morning wood or a sunset.

Lewis's view of Wordsworth

But what do we make of Lewis's view of Wordsworth in the light of this apparent disagreement in their world views? In his essay "Christianity and Literature" in *Christian Reflections*, Lewis calls Wordsworth, ". . . the romantic who made a good end . . " (CR 23). But it would be a mistake to conclude that Wordsworth was a befuddled idealist that Lewis tried to set straight. Lewis was tremendously devoted in his reading of Wordsworth. Lewis would never consent to reread anything he thought poor writing or poor thought. In *An Experiment in Criticism* Lewis defines great literature in part by its power on subsequent re-readings. He cites *The Prelude* as one of the ten most influential works on his thinking. Furthermore, Lewis places Wordsworth on his side in the debate about 'stock responses' in his poem, "A Confession"(CP 15). In addition, in his poem, "To Roy Campbell" he chides Campbell for using "Romanticist" as a derogatory term against "Leftist" writers, saying:

> Newman said much the same of Wordsworth too.
> Now certain critics, far from dear to you,
> May also fondle Wordsworth. But who cares?
> Look at the facts. He's far more ours than theirs;
> Or, if we carve him up, then all that's best
> Falls to our share—we'll let them take the rest.
> By rights the only half they should enjoy
> Is the rude, raw, unlicked, North Country boy. (CP 80-81)

Lewis plainly prefers the aging and orthodox Wordsworth who crafted the final version of *The Prelude* to the young Jacobin radical that flirted with pantheism. Yet Wordsworth's vision rises above these objections. There is, in fact, a spirit in the woods, and no one has done more to burnish this on our hearts than Wordsworth. Simplicity of heart and mind, a quality that MacDonald draws from Wordsworth, is in fact necessary for spiritual growth. There is more wisdom in Wordsworth's dancing lambs and anthropomorphic flowers, if we see them as metaphors, than their apparent simplicity betrays. Notice too that Lewis only faults such imagery if it is taken literally. And if people bring their dark side to the lessons nature teaches through the medium of the imagination, it is because they have willfully misunderstood the message of their Creator. More important, Wordsworth stands as a loud and eloquent voice warning man against pride and the materialist world view that Lewis combated, at a time when the Enlightenment seemed to push away her Creator and embark on the road that led to her becoming Peter Kreeft's "Endarkenment." Lewis may be cautious of embracing all of Wordsworth's optimistic faith in nature, but this is the early Wordsworth after all. Lewis is fully comfortable with the later Wordsworth, "more ours than theirs," and fully comfortable with the 1850 *Prelude*, which is certainly the poet's final statement to the world.

Natural Imagery from *The Prelude*

Regardless of his reluctance to take anything close to a pantheistic view of nature, Lewis's Narnia is a world that owes a lot to the imagery of *The Prelude*. Wordsworth's vision of the beautiful world broadcasting the "Mind and Spirit of the Universe" had great power with the Lewis, who found great pleasure in long country rambles, as had Wordsworth. As stated in a previous chapter, nature in Wordsworth, and ultimately in Lewis, is a mode by which God becomes present to man, and thus by definition, a sacrament. The Anglican *Book of Common Prayer* defines sacrament as, "outward and visible signs of inward and spiritual grace . . . ." (BCP 857). Both Wordsworth and Lewis were deeply Anglican, though both had their times in youth in which they turned their backs on the faith. Wordsworth had his time as a supporter of the secularism of the French Revolution and Lewis had his years of atheism. Yet, as both moved back into the faith, they returned to the Anglican Church. Wordsworth had close family ties to Anglican clergy: his uncle, his brother and his son. He was originally designated by his uncles to become an Anglican clergyman himself. Lewis through his parents on both sides was raised a devout Anglican, and his grandfather was an Anglican clergyman. So undoubtedly, both Wordsworth and Lewis were raised knowing their Anglican catechism. And this very Anglican definition of sacrament, the concept of a visible grace, is found first in Wordsworth's concept of nature and later in Lewis's imagery of the Narnian landscape. Here in this early passage from the first book of *The Prelude* (all quotes will be from the 1850 version, which Lewis knew):

> Fair seed-time had my soul, and I grew up
> Fostered alike by beauty and by fear:
> Much favoured in my birthplace, and no less
> In that beloved Vale to which erelong
> We were transplanted—there were we let loose
> For sports of a wider range. Ere I had told
> Ten birth-days, when among the mountain slopes
> Frost, and the breath of frosty wind, had snapped
> The last autumnal crocus, 'twas my joy
> With store of springes o'er my shoulder hung
> To range the open heights where woodcocks ran
> Along the smooth green turf. (301-312)

The first two books are littered with passages like this. Other examples include:

> We were a noisy crew; the sun in heaven
> Beheld not vales more beautiful than ours;
> Nor saw a ban in happiness and joy
> Richer, or worthier of the ground they trod.
> I could record with no reluctant voice
> The woods of autumn, and their hazel bowers

With milk-white clusters hung; the rod and line,
True symbol of hope's foolishness, whose strong
And unreproved enchantment led us on
By rocks and pools shut out from every star,
All the green summer, to forlorn cascades
Among the windings hid of mountain brooks. (479-490)

Before we compare anything else, here is a tremendous similarity of tone, of a sense of wonder in the glory of the landscape. This, as much as anything else, Lewis manages to transmit into the descriptions of Narnia. As I point out elsewhere, both Wordsworth and Lewis are tremendously enthusiastic walkers and loved what Lewis called the "quiddity" that is, the love of experience for experience's sake, in this case, in nature, whether it be observing a glorious sunset or getting drenched in a rain shower.

In comparison to the above passage, when we first see Narnia in *The Lion, The Witch and the Wardrobe*, it is covered in snow. But then this is Narnia under a cruel enchantment of perpetual winter. Winter, both in Wordsworth's idealized and remembered Lake District and in Narnia, is good as a passing season and only evil when unnaturally prolonged. Lewis balances the negative presentation of winter with the coming of Father Christmas. Wordsworth relates scenes of boys gleefully skating on the lakes. But spring, not winter, is the season of the restoration of life. Thus, our first real view of Narnia is in Aslan's thaw that heralds the beginning of the defeat of the White Witch.

Soon, wherever you looked, instead of white shapes you saw the dark green of firs or the black prickly branches of bare oaks and beeches and elms. Then the mist turned from white to gold and presently cleared away altogether. Shafts of delicious sunlight struck down onto the forest floor and overhead you could see the blue sky between the treetops. . . . a glade of silver birch trees, Edmund saw the ground covered in all directions with little yellow flowers—celandines. The noise of water grew louder. Presently they all crossed a stream. Beyond it they found snowdrops growing. (LWW 97)

These passages are not that close in diction. True, both Wordsworth and Lewis like featuring celandines—Wordsworth wrote at least two poems about them. Yet, it is not Wordsworth's blank verse that is finding its way into Lewis's prose here. What is similar is that both Wordsworth's Cumbria and Lewis's Narnia are green and wooded. This at first may not seem very remarkable. After all, lots of fairy tales and children's stories are set in a wood. And like most tales from the British Isles, the woods are unmistakably British in their flora and fauna. But both in Wordsworth's poem and Lewis's fairy tales, these woods are the location of the spiritual growth of a child or of children. In light of the Romantic view of the importance of the life and perceptions of a child, this is very significant. For Lewis, Narnia is a compilation of all the things that delight him: beautiful countryside, a prosperous and pre-industrial medieval culture, talking animals, dwarves from Norse mythology, satyrs, fauns and centaurs from Greek mythology, and the site for Edith Nesbitt type children's adventures. But it is more than just that. Here Edmund, just to mention one case, turns from a nasty little brat into a noble king. It is the location of spiritual growth, of gaining one's true face. As with the presence of Aslan, everything comes right, so with the influence of Aslan, people come right, come into being what they were born to be. War refugees become kings and queens. Eustace becomes a dragon, which he has been in fact all along, only so that he can ultimately be un-dragoned. A bullied, trembling school girl becomes the Lady Jill Pole, rescuer of King Rilian the Disenchanted, and warrior in the Last Battle of Narnia.

For Wordsworth too, this is a central theme. *The Prelude* is a long, poetic explanation by Wordsworth to Coleridge and the whole world, how his experiences, including his childhood in the woods, have come to make him a poet. Though a good deal of *The Prelude* takes place in Cambridge, France or London, the segments where Wordsworth is healed and made a poet primarily take place in the Lake District. For both Lewis and Wordsworth, woods are the hatchery of the true soul of a human being. Nor is this arbitrary. Woods have always had mysterious connotations. In Celtic mythology they were holy places where spiritual powers are hidden and to be sought. For both Lewis and Wordsworth woods and meadows take on this role. For Lewis the woods are the place one meets Aslan, and if the woods seem full and larger than life, it is because some adventure awaits us that will eventually lead us to Aslan, or around the next tree trunk may be Aslan Himself. The woods dance to awaken as Lucy, awakened from a dream, wanders through them to see Aslan himself (PC 113).

The woods, in the definition given above, are a kind of sacrament— they are the place where Heaven leaks through to our mundane reality. For Wordsworth, ever wary of making a definite statement of anything like theology, the sense is there but it is always vague:

> Wisdom and Spirit of the universe!
> Thou Soul that art the eternity of thought,
> That givest to forms and image a breath
> And everlasting motion, not in vain

By day or star-light thus from my first dawn
Of childhood didn't thou intertwine for me
The passions that build up our human soul;
But with high objects, with enduring things—
With life and nature, purifying thus
The elements of feeling and of thought,
And sanctifying, by such discipline,
Both pain and fear, until we recognise
A grandeur in the beatings of the heart. (I. 401-414)

For Wordsworth, the woods bring him somehow (he will not say exactly how) to the very borders of something like Heaven. For Lewis, Heaven is a stable doorway away.

The Vision of Heaven—
The Last Battle and *The Silver Chair*

In the Narnia stories, Lewis is creating his vision of Heaven and that vision is especially aware of the glory of nature. Like Wordsworth, he is in fact drawing from his own memories and experience. Heaven in *The Last Battle* is basically Narnia only more so. When Tirian, having been thrust through the stable door, finally takes in the landscape of Aslan's Country around him, he sees,

> In reality they stood on grass, the deep blue sky was overhead, and the air which blew gently on their face was that of a day in early summer. Not far away from them rose a grove of trees, thickly leaved, but under every leaf there peeped out the gold or faint yellow or purple or glowing red of fruits such as no one has seen in our world. The fruit made Tirian feel that it must be autumn; but there was something in the feel of the air that told him it could not be later than June. (LB 128)

This is the second time in the Narnia series we have witnessed Lewis's Heaven, or Aslan's Country. The first time is two brief sections in *The Silver Chair* where Jill and Eustace enter the world containing Narnia by first entering a corner of Heaven, that is, Aslan's Country.

> Instantly there was a quite different sound all about them. It came from those bright things overhead, which now turned out to be birds. They were making riotous noise, but it was much more like music—rather advanced music which you don't quite take in at the first hearing—than birds' songs ever are in our world. Yet, in spite of the singing, there was a sort of background of immense silence. That silence, combined with the

freshness of the air, made Jill think they must be on the top of a very high mountain.

Scrubb still had her by the hand and they were walking forward, staring about them on every side. Jill saw that huge trees, rather like cedars but bigger, grew in every direction. But as they did not grow close together, and as there was no undergrowth, this did not prevent one from seeing a long way into the forest to left and right. And as far as Jill's eye could reach, it was all the same—level turf, darting birds with yellow or dragonfly blue or rainbow plumage, blue shadows, and emptiness. There was not a breath of wind in that cool, bright air. It was a very lonely forest. (SC 10)

Here too the country is green and wooded and it is a sunny day and there is a stream from which Jill must drink. There also is openness, a total lack of crowding which we associate with our busy urban lives. Yet, for Lewis, who loved the university as well as the open woods, the ideal place would be a mixture of both.

In a quote in a *C.S. Lewis Centenary Group Internet Newsletter* of 16 March 1998, the Right Honourable David Bleakley recalls a conversation with Lewis from Bleakley's student days in Oxford.

On one of our walks (he asked) what was my idea of Heaven. I tried hard to put some definition together, but he soon interrupted my theological meanderings. "My friend, you are far too complicated; an honest Ulsterman living in Oxford should know better. Surely, David, Heaven is Oxford lifted and placed in the middle of County Down.

Douglas Gresham has confirmed that Lewis modeled the landscape of Narnia on County Down (Gresham). So essentially, Lewis's image of both Narnia and Heaven is Ireland in terms of flora and fauna. This is not to say that Lewis held this position dogmatically, as some sort of theological fact. I believe he would have said that this was the most beautiful image he could project and if this were not true, something better would be. What is noteworthy about this choice of image is that Lewis was a student of Medieval and Renaissance literature. Before the Romantics, Heaven was traditionally urban: the central image, borrowed from the book of Revelation, was of Jerusalem, the City of God. Likewise, untamed nature, or wilderness, was a place of temptation for both Jesus and the Children of Israel. For anyone not familiar with this concept, the American novel, *The Scarlet Letter* by Nathaniel Hawthorne, gives a vivid picture of the common pre-Romantic notion of nature. The woods are where the savage Indians, pagan children of the devil live.

Wordsworth and the Romantics, seeing the industrial revolution turn cities into teeming slums where people withered in bleak poverty, reversed this image. God was found in Nature and the city became a bleak sort of hell as presented in literature, the location of Blake's "Dark, Satanic mills." Even though he is a student of the Middle Ages and the Renaissance, it is noteworthy that Lewis casts Heaven in a Romantic image as opposed to a pre-Romantic image of the kind he would have been most familiar with in the literature in which he was a professed expert. In fact, we see very little of any city in the whole of the Narnia series. Cair Paravel has a castle, we know. Beaversdam is a village, though as Aslan passes through it in *Prince Caspian*, he wreaks havoc, destroying bridges and demolishing at least one house. Narnia is primarily a country of fauns and animals dancing in moonlight clearings and dwarves working in mountain caves. It is decidedly, and by Aslan's own indicated will, a rural country. Indeed, the certain sign of moral evil among the Telmarines of *Prince Caspian* is their fear of woods, an attitude that would have been familiar in pre-Romantic Britain and all of Europe. And as Narnia is destroyed in *The Last Battle*, it is by Calormenes busily engaged in utilizing Narnian natural resources, brutally logging her woods in a very modern industrial, mass-harvesting sort of way.

But Lewis, like Wordsworth, enjoyed long walking tours through the fields and woods of England and Wales with his brother and other friends as Wordsworth enjoyed walks with his friends and family. His love of a known landscape permeates the Narnia stories so powerfully that the reader cannot help but share it. Lewis in a few words makes the place itself as vivid as Wordsworth has made the Lake District.

The Image of the Mountain in the Vision of Heaven

We can observe a similar development in Lewis's imagery going further back to *The Pilgrim's Regress*. The pilgrim, John, is drawn by the vision of a distant mountain surrounded by sea. At a distance, John cannot see it clearly, but he smells the scent of "sweet orchards" from the mountain's side (PR 171-2). He finds out that the mountain is the "Landlord's" country, and that he must reverse his journey to go toward it. And, of course, it is wooded with at least some of fruit tree that gives off a pleasant scent. The image of the mountain of Heaven returns again in *The Great Divorce* when the narrator-ghost arrives in the bright country. After discovering his own transparency, the narrator-ghost looks up at the center of the Heavenly country:

Greenness and light had almost swallowed them [the other ghosts] up. But very far away I could see a range of mountains. Sometimes I could make out in it steep forests, far-withdrawing valleys, and even mountain cities perched on inaccessible summits. At other times it became indistinct. The height was so enormous that my waking sight could not have taken in such an object at all. Light brooded on the top of it: slanting down thence it made long shadows behind every tree on the plain. . . . . A tiny haze and a sweet smell went up where they [the bright people of Heaven] had crushed the grass and scattered the dew. (GD 29-30)

Once again, the intensely wooded mountain is the home of God Himself. The light in the above image flows eternally from God himself, and thus there is no moving sun to change the shadows. This is directly from the New Testament, "And night shall be no more; they need no light of lamp or sun, for the Lord God will be their light, and they shall reign for ever and ever" (Rev 22:5 RSV).

When we are in Aslan's Country in *The Silver Chair*, Jill and Eustace are confronted with a cliff at the edge of it, which is described as incredibly tall in one of Lewis's better passages of description.

Imagine yourself at the top of the very highest cliff you know. And imagine yourself looking down to the very bottom. And then imagine that the precipice goes on below that, as far again, ten times as far, twenty times as far. And when you've looked down all that distance, imagine little white things that might, at first glance, be mistaken for sheep, but presently you realize that they are clouds—not little wreaths of mist but the enormous white, puffy clouds which are themselves as big as most mountains. And at last, in between those clouds, you get your first glimpse of the real bottom, so far away that you can't make out whether it's field or wood, or land or water: further below those clouds than you are above them. (SC 11)

There are two important things to notice here. First, as neither any of us, the living, nor Lewis has ever seen Heaven, he is forced to cite the most heavenly landscape he knows and then telescope on it. So he has done here, by asking the reader to recall the highest cliff they know and then telescope on the image. Second, we are once again on top of a mountain for Aslan's Country. In *The Voyage of the Dawn Treader* at the end, we are allowed to see the same view from the bottom up at the moment before Reepicheep takes his coracle into Aslan's Country.

What they saw—eastward, beyond the sun—was a range of mountains. It was so high that either they never saw the top of it or they forgot it. None of them remembers seeing any sky in that direction. And the mountains must really have been outside the world. For any mountains even a quarter of a twentieth of that height ought to have had ice and snow on them. But these were warm and green and full of forests and waterfalls however high you looked. . . . . No one in that boat doubted that they were seeing beyond the end of the world into Aslan's country. (VDT 205-6)

When in the last Narnia book, the Pevensies, Tirian and their party leave destroyed Narnia behind, they are encouraged by Aslan to move "Further up and further in." "In" is upward in Lewis's Heaven, up to the top of the mountain. And that final dash for the heart of Aslan's Country, up where the light comes from God Himself, is the culmination of the Narnia series.

Though Wordsworth is not writing fantasy and though he does not claim it as Heaven, his encounter with nature throughout *The Prelude* changes him and causes him to grow as the protagonists of the Narnia stories grow in each of the seven tales. Wordsworth's final moment of full and final realization of his calling as a poet and as a human being comes on an ascent of Mt. Snowdon in North Wales. The ascent takes place in the dark early morning hours so that as Wordsworth and his companions clear the fog, they come out into the pale light of the full moon. Wordsworth looks out at the scattered mountain tops around them, like islands in the sea of fog that blankets the valleys and the lower slopes of the mountain, and launches into several ecstatic pages of blank verse that culminate in his encountering Raisley Calvert (who funded his early poetic career) and Coleridge, and the beginnings of his years as a poet. He concludes from his vision:

> When into air had partially dissolved
> That vision, given to spirits of the night
> And three chance human wanderers, in calm thought
> Reflected, it appeared to me the type
> Of a majestic intellect, its acts
> And its possessions, what it has and craves,
> What in itself it is, and would become.
> There I beheld the emblem of a mind
> That feeds upon infinity, that broods
> Over the dark abyss, intent to hear
> Its voice issuing forth to silent light
> In one continuous stream; a mind sustained
> By recognitions of transcendent power,
> In sense conducting to ideal form,
> In soul of more than mortal privilege. (14. 63-77)

This passage, even in this last and most overtly Christian version of *The Prelude*, is a classic example of how Wordsworth can talk at length about his sense of experiencing God in great intensity but demurring from coming right out and naming Him. The allusion in line 71 to the Holy Spirit brooding in Milton's *Paradise Lost* argues strongly for this passage to be about God. Modern critics tend to avoid the question. But the Miltonian allusion is fairly conclusive. I have edited the passage at line 77, when in fact it rambles in this ecstasy until at least line 129, making other allusions along the way. Though the critical consensus is not absolute, for the sake of argument, let us assume that Wordsworth is referring to what Lewis would have called a "numinous" experience of God. Indeed, any other interpretation seems to me a severe strain and a rather long reach. But Lewis, re-reading this poem year after year, through the eyes of faith, would inevitably have seen these lines as an experience of God. And it is Lewis's reading of *The Prelude* that concerns us here. And this is the point, that at the apex of Wordsworth's journey to being a poet, he is standing in the presence of God Himself on the top of a mountain. Wordsworth's most ecstatic and deeply religious lines of poetry perhaps, pour out of him upon seeing the creation below him, where the fog looks like a sea in the moonlight and the mountaintops like islands in this fantastic "ethereal" (line 50) world so unlike our everyday world. It is this image which we see echoed in Lewis's vision of Heaven, though the moonlight has turned to bright sun and the bare slopes of Snowdon to the green meadows and woods of Aslan's Mountain. It is this image of Heaven which we see in Lewis and not the urban "City of God."

Lucy, the Wordsworthian Child in Heaven

Of course, when thinking of the name "Lucy" and Wordsworth, we immediately think of the Lucy poems written in Goslar in the winter of 1798-9. Lucy in these poems is an elusive figure, innocent and lost to death more often than not. She is a symbol of innocence, untouchable and lost in time and shrouded in a kind of tragic grief. It is most likely that Lewis chose the name of his young heroine because he was thinking not of Wordsworth's Lucy, but of Lucy Barfield, his godchild, to whom he dedicated *The Lion, the Witch and the Wardrobe*. The only commonality between the two Lucies is their innocence, but that may be all that Lewis intended for his Lucy. The Wordsworthian connection is much more potent in terms of the dimensions of that innocence than the simple coincidence of the character names.

In his poem, "Ode: Intimations of Immortality," Wordsworth says of the child:

Not in entire forgetfulness,
And not in utter nakedness,
But trailing clouds of glory do we come
From God, who is our home:
Heaven lies about us in our infancy!
Shades of the prison-house begin to close
Upon the growing Boy
But He beholds the light, and whence it flows,
He sees it in his joy;
The Youth, who daily farther from the east
Must travel, still is Nature's Priest. (PW 460)

This idea of the value of becoming like a little child in order to enter the Kingdom of Heaven pre-dates the Romantics and goes back to the words of Christ. However, it's the Romantics who singularly possessed by it. For Wordsworth, the child is Nature's Priest. And as Wordsworth rarely used words sloppily and was a life-long Anglican, we can perhaps take that phrase to mean that for Wordsworth, the child to some degree has the sacramental duty of a priest to be a conduit of the grace found in nature. Certainly for MacDonald this was so. Curdie, Gibbie and so many other innocent but true shepherd boy characters by their innocence, character and virtue bless all around them. In fact, nature in Wordsworth, and ultimately in Lewis, is a mode by which God becomes present to man, and thus by definition, a sacrament, "outward and visible signs of inward and spiritual grace . . . " (BCP 857).

In Narnia, it is Lucy Pevensie who is a very Wordsworthian sort of child. She is the youngest of the four and has that innocence of youth that even as she grows older she never quite loses. For Wordsworth and the Romantics, the more childlike one is, the closer one is to Heaven. This is a perfect description of Lucy. One gets a sense also that her being feminine to Aslan's masculinity has something to do with it too. But it is Lucy that Aslan appears to most often and usually first. It is Lucy who is most eager to rescue Tumnus and to meet Aslan; it is Lucy who senses Aslan's pain and with Susan longs to accompany him to his death at the Stone Table. It is Lucy who almost drags the fearful Susan through trying to untie him. It is Lucy who sees Aslan when the others can't and so leads them to Aslan's How in time to rescue Caspian's army. Edmund, in explaining to Eustace who Aslan is, admits, "We've all seen him. Lucy sees him most often." (VDT 91) It is Lucy, who even as she is being told by Aslan that she is now too old to return to Narnia, blurts out to Aslan with her childlike purity of heart, "It isn't Narnia, you know, . . . It's you. We shan't meet you there. And how can we live, never meeting you?" (VDT 209). Aslan assures her that she will find him in our world, though by another name. And in *The Last Battle*, standing in Aslan's Country explaining to King Tirian what has happened, we see that Lucy has made the connection, before anyone else can speak it.

> "Yes," said Queen Lucy. "In our world too a stable once had something inside it that was bigger than our whole world." It was the first time she had spoken, and from the thrill in her voice Tirian now knew why. She was drinking everything in more deeply than the others. She had been too happy to speak. (LB 133)

It is Lucy who has realized before anyone else that the lion and the child in the manger at Bethlehem are one in the same, and that they have reached Aslan's Country, and in the depth of her love for him, she is overwhelmed with happiness. And as 'Nature's Priest,' she is first to communicate this grace with her fellows. Yes, there is a spirit in the woods, and his name, or one of his names, is Aslan. We cannot miss in Wordsworth's poems or Jack Lewis's Narnia, or even MacDonald's fairy tales and novels, this great all-pervading feeling of emanating goodness coming into the world from this spirit in the woods that outweighs every sorrow. This draw of desire through nature's beauty from just beyond the margins of the world calls through the work of all three writers.

CHAPTER FIVE

PERELANDRA AND THE SPACE TRILOGY: CREATION AND THE MEDIEVAL UTOPIA IN LEWIS'S VISION

Veldman's Argument

Next to R.J. Reilly's *Romantic Religion*, the most thorough and illuminating study of Lewis's Romanticism does not even focus on Lewis. It is by Louisiana State University historian Meredith Veldman, *Fantasy, the Bomb and the Greening of Britain: Romantic Protest 1945-1980*. Veldman convincingly argues that the response of Tolkien and Lewis to the empiricism of their age and industrialization was in all essentials Romantic. She goes on to argue that the anti-nuclear movement and the "Green" environmental movement in Britain owe a great deal of their origins to that same love of the natural and the pre-industrial medieval world we see both in Tolkien's Shire and Lewis's Narnia. Like William Morris before them, they connect the pre-industrial idealized agrarian world with the British medieval world. According to Veldman, "Lewis used his fantastic re-creation of the medieval model to illuminate the failings of twentieth-century society. The medieval model had provided a coherent cosmos, a world in which humanity and nature were linked in and unbreakable chain" (Veldman 1994, 64). She defines clearly Lewis's view of nature as seen in *Perelandra*:

> Lewis sought to highlight not only God's intended harmony between humanity and nature but also the sanctity of nature itself, apart from any relationship with humanity. Nature, in Lewis's view, is not simply a script in which the Christian reads the drama of God's actions. Nature reveals God to humanity, but this natural revelation is not nature's reason for being. Like many ecologists two decades later, Lewis asserted nature's right to exist, its holiness as a living entity, apart from its utility to humanity. Man's appropriation of nature as a thing, rather than respect for it as a fellow creation, violates the divine plan. (65)

These two principles are central to Lewis's view of nature: first, nature is our fellow creature, and should be neither exploited nor deified. And second, she should therefore be respected. The first point Lewis makes in several places, but notably in *Miracles*.

> . . . only Supernaturalists really see Nature. You must go a little way from her, and then turn round, and look back. Then at last the true landscape will become visible . . . . To treat her as God, or as Everything, is to lose the whole pith and pleasure of her. Come out, look back, and then you will see this astonishing cataract of bears, babies, and bananas: this immoderate deluge of atoms, orchids, oranges, cancers, canaries, fleas, gases, tornadoes and toads. . . .She is herself. Offer her neither worship nor contempt. (M 66)

He likewise says cautiously: "Nature never taught me that there exists a God of glory and of infinite majesty. . . . . But nature gave the word glory a meaning for me. I do not know where else I could have found one" (FL 37). It is this balanced delight in nature that does not grasp after the experience, that we find in *Perelandra*.

Perelandra as Unfallen Nature: the Temptation of Technological Magic

Perelandra is probably, outside of the scenery in Narnia, Lewis's most powerful fictional statement on nature. It is perhaps the strongest of the science fiction trilogy, and yet there is so little that is scientific about it that we might call it science fiction. Outside of Weston's arrival by space ship, there is nothing mechanical nor especially scientific in the novel. The universe that Ransom and Weston travel through is not the Outer Space of so many contemporary science fiction novels but the Heavens of medieval cosmology which Lewis defined in his scholarly book *The Discarded Image*. As Veldman has discerned, this is a story about the natural world approached from a Romantic perspective. Perhaps it would be better classified as a supernatural and Romantic space fantasy. Lewis the anti-vivisectionist is presenting us with a natural world in which we must learn to respect our fellow creation.

One of the many evils that Weston/Satan/the Unman perpetrates is the senseless murder of small singing frogs. Indeed, Unman destroys whenever possible: "A great deal of his [Ransom's] time was spent in protecting the animals from it [the Unman]. Whenever it got out of sight, or even a few yards ahead, it would make a grab at any beast or bird within its reach and pull out some fur or feathers" (P 129). Unman is bent on the un-making of paradise and the de-glorifying of creation. He also symbolizes the dominance of human technology, of industrialization as he lectures Ransom on the need for humanity to conquer other worlds. Unman in many ways is the very antithesis of Romanticism. As Veldman has seen, the prospective fall of Perelandra involves an abuse of nature. Unman asks the Perelandran Eve to become mistress of her world and not just the subject of Maleldil (God), by disobeying the command not to spend the night on the fixed land. This is the essential motivation behind the advance of technology: to rule nature by force and by godlike will; to make men gods. And after all, this is the original temptation of the Eve of this Earth in the original Garden of Eden. This is the same temptation as the temptation of evil magic, the temptation to Digory of eating the apple of eternal youth and being godlike in *The Magician's Nephew*. Lewis understood that the distance between black magic and immoral use of scientific knowledge was not very great.

Elsewhere Lewis connects this desire with the notion that science will liberate us from nature. In *The Abolition of Man* he states, "For the wise men of old the cardinal problem had been how to conform the soul to reality, and the solution had been knowledge, self-discipline and virtue. For magic and applied science alike the problem is how to subdue reality to the wishes of men" (AM 87-8). This becomes problematic, as in Weston's philosophy, which Lewis is attacking in essay form in *The Abolition of Man*, to subdue nature ultimately means for some people to exercise technological power over the rest of humanity. Lewis calls them "Conditioners." But as those Conditioners are ultimately human and subject to their impulses and appetites, they are subject also, like it or not, to nature. In Lewis's phrase, "Man's conquest of Nature turns out, in the moment of its consummation, to be Nature's conquest of Man" (AM 80). Unman's philosophy is ultimately futile and, of course, an irrational attempt to turn Perelandra into the kind of hell Earth can often be. And, as Ransom discovers, there is no answer for Unman's endless droning temptation but to destroy the tempter. Ransom's victory over Unman is the rescue of unfallen nature on Perelandra. In some respects it parallels Wordsworth's rescue from despair over the futility of his youthful political idealism and his restoration to moral and mental health by the good offices of Coleridge, his sister, and the beauty of nature all around him in Devon and later on, the Lake District.

The Triple Pattern of Growth in Edenic Places

Although *Perelandra* definitely owes far more influence to Milton's *Paradise Lost* than any other work of literature, there is an interesting pattern to be found in the narrative episodes that echoes the pattern found in *The Prelude*. This is not something intentional; Lewis did not set out to re-create *The Prelude* in the sense that he in *Perelandra* is playing with Milton's story. This is a result of Lewis's imbibing the woof and warp of *The Prelude* by reading it "umpteen times" (Sayer 245). But though we find grandeur of landscape and, if you will, heaven-scape in *Paradise Lost*, Milton does not share Lewis's view of nature as Veldman has so succinctly defined it above. This Lewis shares with Wordsworth and the Romantics.

The pattern we see in both Wordsworth's *Prelude* and Lewis's *Perelandra* is in three stages of a journey: first, the journeyer is thrown into nature from which he learns valuable lessons. Second, the journeyer must face severe trials that remake his understanding of the journey and reform his character. The third stage is when the journeyer triumphs over adversity and finds his place in the universe.

In the first stage in *The Prelude*, Wordsworth's autobiographical narrator recalls the life and adventures of his childhood, in Lewis's words, quoted above, that of a "rude, raw, unlicked north country boy." Wordsworth's boy child both glories in nature and abuses it, bird-nesting and stealing rowboats. But nature acts like a conscience to him and teaches him via the spots of time, lessons on humanity, and the proper respect of nature. Ransom never abuses nature and is a grown man when he arrives in Perelandra. But his womb-like clear coffin that carries him from Earth to Venus, or Perelandra is symbolically a rebirth. Though he is tempted to abuse his setting by indulging in the popping of the bubbles that refresh him, he quickly learns a respect for nature in this new world.

The second stage of the journey in *The Prelude* is Wordsworth's going to school, to Cambridge University, and his travels through revolutionary France. This stage includes the central books of *The Prelude*, books 3 through 11, which also detail his attempts at reform in London and his profound discouragement when the British Government suppressed reform and declared war on revolutionary France. In Book 12 he details how with the help of his sister Dorothy and his friend, Coleridge, his confidence was restored and he found his vocation as a poet.

Ransom's second stage begins with his verbal battle with Unman and intensifies with the physical battle in which Ransom barehanded does his best to destroy Unman and succeeds only after a long and costly fight.

The third and final stage in Wordsworth's poem is the last book, Book 14, in which Wordsworth climbs Mt. Snowdon in the moonlight and has an ecstatic realization of his purpose and place within nature. Ransom likewise is taken to the meeting of the King and Queen, the Adam and Eve of Perelandra, where he too becomes aware of an ecstatic vision of the Great Dance in which he sees not only his place, but the place of all beings within the universe.

Indeed, Tirian in *The Last Battle* goes through just such a journey of youth, trial and triumph. In the opening of the novel, Tirian makes two rash decisions which end with his having dissipated what military strength he could have mustered and being taken captive by the invading Calormenes. At the beginning of this sequence he is relaxing with his friend, Jewel the Unicorn. The image here is of a king not on guard as his country is imperiled by a threat that he could not have imagined. Armies arriving from the south or giants mustering in the north are things this king knows of, for the text tells us that the king and Jewel had saved each other in battle before. Subversion inside the country is something unforeseen. This is the sort of mistake that youth can commonly make, lacking experience to deal with unusual threats.

The second stage is when Tirian fights his doomed campaign to regain control of Narnia against the false Aslan and the Calormenes. Tirian does not win, but what is more important, with little hope he stands up for the right. The third stage is not so much Tirian's triumph, but Aslan's, when the destruction and enslavement of Narnia causes the end of the Narnian world and Tirian finds himself a guest forever in Aslan's Country.

So, in this threefold pattern, Wordsworth justifies his calling as the poet of nature by his childhood, by his long wandering in the wilderness of university life and revolutionary politics, and by his transformation and return to nature during his moonlit hike on Snowdon. Ransom fulfills his calling by his long womblike journey across space, by his openness to the new and strange (to him) nature of this new world, by his long and costly combat and by his vision of the Great Dance. However, unlike Wordsworth, Lewis views nature as in need of redemption as well, at least nature as it is twisted on earth.

True Edenic Balance in Wordsworth and Lewis: Adam Shall Rule and Name the Beasts

Nature, however, on Perelandra is unfallen, and therefore as idyllic as it is in Wordsworth's poetry. The redemption of nature is secured by Ransom's sacrifice. So thus here in *Perelandra*, Lewis is able to put aside for a few pages the caution against seeing nature as something godlike and possibly pantheistic, something that he faulted Wordsworth for doing. Here nature, symbolized in part by the perfect Adam and Eve of Perelandra, is in total harmony with this new breed of humanity. All nature is in harmony with the King and Queen. We see this in the way that the animals respond to the Queen, following her with adoration and even laughing when she laughs at Ransom in his "piebald" skin caused by selective tanning. When the victory over Unman is complete, Ransom is brought before the King and Queen to witness what Earth never has: unfallen humanity in perfect harmony with creation, Adam and Eve justly and kindly ruling and naming the beasts. It is an image that Lewis was fond of, and repeated in *The Magician's Nephew* in the crowning of King Frank and Queen Helen on the first day of Narnia, ruling and naming the beasts of Narnia. It is also briefly repeated in *The Great Divorce* where one of the bright spirits arrives with animals dancing joyfully around her. It was, for Lewis, one of the most concrete images of paradise.

CHAPTER SIX

SURPRISED BY JOY AND THE REDEMPTION OF NATURE

No study of Lewis's Romanticism would be complete without examining *Surprised by Joy*. As has already been stated above, the issue of *Sehnsucht*, or joy, has been thoroughly done elsewhere, and though I readily concede its primary importance, the business of the book is to look at the other elements of Lewis's Romanticism and examine them. The most outstanding feature here is the almost ambivalent attitude Lewis holds towards nature.

Lewis on one hand is sternly vigilant against the possibility of making nature a god, or simply God. He labels this "pantheistic mysticism" (CR 16) and contrasts it with "innocent sensuousness." This pantheistic mysticism is what is often referred to as "Nature Religion" and associated with the modern New Age Movement. Lewis views nature differently. She is first our fellow creature, as was demonstrated in the previous chapter. Thus she deserves our respect as Ransom learns and practices on Perelandra. Second, nature may transmit the glory of God, or at least acquaint us with the concept. It may give us the sense of the numinous. But if we stop there, our religion becomes one of convenience and amoral. Not even Wordsworth saw nature in such a vague and pantheistic way. In *Mere Christianity*, Lewis relates this problem by telling of an RAF officer who doubted the validity of theology but knew there was a god because, "I've *felt* Him: out alone in the desert at night: the tremendous mystery" (MC 119). Lewis's response is that the officer's felt experience is valid but it does not allow anyone to know God or respond to Him in any significant way. In fact, it is rather a dodge: all the mysticism of nature-inspired theism with none of the worries of a God who cares about you or what you might do. Lewis argues that theology, that is, the dogma of revealed Christianity, is like a map. The experience of crossing the ocean will necessarily be more real, but one needs the map to cross the ocean nevertheless. Without it, religion is, "all thrills and no work; like watching the waves from the beach" (MC 120).

Lewis's more dire warning against this pantheistic mysticism is found in *The Four Loves* and part of this was quoted in the first chapter. In the chapter titled "Likings and Love for the Sub-Human," after criticizing Wordsworth for seeing too much in nature, Lewis warns that the lessons of nature might not only be beauty and the transcendent God behind nature, but the "dark gods of the blood" and perhaps even ruthless, social Darwinist competition. Then Lewis goes on to qualify this apparently dark assessment:

> [In nature] We have seen an image of glory. We must not try to find a direct path through it and beyond it to an increasing knowledge of God. The path peters out almost at once. . . . We must make a detour—leave the hills and woods and go back to our studies, to church, to our Bibles, to our knees. Otherwise the love of nature is beginning to turn into a nature religion. And then, even if it does not lead us to the Dark Gods, it will lead us to a great deal of nonsense.
>
> But we need not surrender the love of nature—chastened and limited as I have suggested—to the debunkers. Nature cannot satisfy the desires she arouses nor answer theological questions nor sanctify us. Our real journey to God involves constantly turning our backs on here; passing from the dawn-lit fields to work in an East End parish. But the love of her has been a valuable and, for some people, an indispensable initiation.
>
> I need not say "has been." For in fact those who allow no more than this to the love of nature seem to be those who retain it. This is what one should expect. This love, when it sets up as a religion, is beginning to be a god—therefore a demon. And demons never keep their promises. Nature "dies" on those who try to live for a love of nature. Coleridge ended by being insensible to her; Wordsworth, by lamenting that a glory had passed away. Say your prayers in a garden early, ignoring steadfastly the dew, the birds and the flowers, and you will come away overwhelmed by its freshness and joy; go there in order to be overwhelmed and, after a certain age, nine times out of ten nothing will happen to you.(FL 38-9)

There are several things compacted into this long passage that I want to address. First, Lewis maintains almost a fear of nature worship that might become pantheism or unbridled and cruel sensuality. Still, though Lewis is cynical as to what one might learn from, in Wordsworth's words, "an impulse in a vernal wood," he is still committed to the knowledge that what one can best learn is a glimpse of the glory of God. To this sacramental function of nature he applies the Principal of Inattention, and corollary of Christ's injunction that the only way to keep something is to give it away; that is for Lewis, that we must not try and indulge in what he calls in *Surprised by Joy* "temple-making." We cannot grasp God in the beauty of nature. It is only a preview. The reality is as mundane as a parish church in the East End of London. And as we have said before, for Lewis, nature, beauty, and joy are very fine things, as long as we recognize them as Second Things and not First Things.

The final thing to be noted here is that, uncharacteristic of the literary scholar he was, his account of Wordsworth and Coleridge's end is not accurate. Coleridge never based his beliefs on "an impulse in the vernal wood"; Coleridge was always religious, and criticized Godwin and Thelwell and other radicals of the time for trying to envision a revolution without faith. Certainly in his youth he was a devout Unitarian and only later on did he come to orthodoxy. But he adamantly all his life felt that Christ was at the center of all things and enjoyed walks through the beauty of Hampstead Heath through the final years of his life. Wordsworth, by the account of his letters, enjoyed the beauty of his home well past the publication of the "Immortality Ode" which Lewis quotes in the above passage. As one can see from the letter quoted in the second chapter, neither was Wordsworth the pantheist Lewis thinks him to be. Wordsworth died at age at 80 because he'd been out walking in nature as he'd always loved to do and got caught in a rainstorm and contracted pleurisy. In fact, Coleridge and Wordsworth are closer to Lewis than Lewis perhaps knew. There again, this may be because Wordsworth was so thoroughly assimilated by MacDonald and Lewis assimilates MacDonald without recognizing or perhaps acknowledging the source of some of MacDonald's concepts.

Lewis repeats this error when he writes:

> There is an easy transition from Theism to Pantheism; but there is also a blessed transition in the other direction. For some souls, I believe, for my own I remember, Wordsworthian contemplation can be the first and lowest form of recognition that there is something outside ourselves that demands reverence. . . . for the 'man coming up from below' the Wordsworthian experience is an advance. (CR 22)

What he says is certainly true, but Wordsworth never committed himself to that sort of pantheism.

The story of Lewis's natural experiences leading to joy in *Surprised by Joy* has been thoroughly traced before. Warren's garden on the tin box lid (SBJ 7) and all that follows are almost common knowledge to readers of Lewis, so I shall not repeat them here. A large part of Lewis's experiences of joy comes through nature experiences (SBJ 77, 78, 118, 152). What's notable is that Lewis is the one coming up through pantheism to theism, and admits so in the passage quoted above. For Lewis, nature did in fact operate as a sacrament that led him to faith. It was certainly not the only element; his love of myth had at least as much if not more influence. But it was one of the steps he climbed.

At the end of *Surprised by Joy*, Lewis seems to discount joy, now that he has faith. This is probably nothing more than his practice of the principle of inattention.

> But what, in conclusion, of Joy? for that, after all, is what the story has mainly been about. To tell you the truth, the subject has lost nearly all interest for me since I became a Christian. I cannot, indeed, complain, like Wordsworth, that the visionary gleam has passed away. I believe (if the thing were at all worth recording) that the old stab, the old bittersweet, has come to me as often and as sharply since my conversion as at any time of my life whatever. But I now know that the experience, considered as a state of my own mind, had never had the kind of importance I once gave it. It was valuable only as a pointer to something other and outer. (SBJ 238)

Certainly the Principle of Inattention is at work here, and if he says he's lost interest, it is intellectual interest only. The fact is, he admits joy strikes him just as often. Yet, he recognizes it as a Second Thing, and therefore does not give it undue attention. But more to the point, from the Sayer biography and other accounts, we know that Lewis, like Wordsworth in the Lake District and Coleridge on Hampstead Heath, continued to be a walker in nature for as long as his health allowed him. His joy in nature did not become a thing of the past after his conversion. Nor are any of Wordsworth's statements about visionary gleams or glory passing away the end of Wordsworth's interest in the beauty of the English countryside. Wordsworth's experience is closer to Lewis's than Lewis knew.

Indeed, Lewis firmly believed that nature was to be redeemed along with the human race. Nature, or at least the good and beautiful aspects of nature, will be a part of Heaven just as our resurrected bodies will be. We have already seen how Aslan's Country and Narnia are a compilation of all that is beautiful in nature to Lewis: the green mountains and graceful woods, images that are found in the first books of *The Prelude*. Lewis writes:

> Christian teaching by saying that God made the world and called it good teaches that Nature or environment cannot be simply irrelevant to spiritual beatitude in general, ... By teaching the resurrection of the body it teaches that Heaven is not merely a state of the spirit but a state of the body as well: and there a state of Nature as a whole. (M 161-2)

In the thought of Lewis, there in Aslan's Country, all that was shoddy about us will burn away or will have already burned away. As Tirian and Jill find themselves in clean and beautiful clothes the moment they enter Aslan's Country, so will humanity be cleaned and clothed.

Wordsworth did not dwell as Lewis did on Heaven. But he did dwell on what he found heavenly on earth. And in his *Prelude*, he dwells on all the joy and agony he passed through in order to become a poet. Lewis is not ignorant of the journey of conversion pattern, for we see it repeatedly, not only in his *Surprised by Joy*, but in the journeys of many of his characters. In Lewis's work, human individuals are on a quest to find not themselves, that is the selves they think they are, but the selves that God designed them to be from before time. In *Till We Have Faces* Lewis writes of the conversion process as being fully clothed in the resurrection body. Then only can man look in unbroken gaze on the face of God Himself. Till we have our true faces, Orual asks, how can we speak to God face to face?

CHAPTER SEVEN

EARLY AND LATE:
THE PILGRIM'S REGRESS
TO *TILL WE HAVE FACES*

We are going to look at two different books by Lewis, *The Pilgrim's Regress*, written not very long after his conversion to Christianity, and *Till We Have Faces*, the last fiction Lewis ever wrote. *The Pilgrim's Regress* is subtitled, "An Allegorical Apology for Christianity, Reason and Romanticism." In the preface, Lewis writes of his use of the word Romanticism in the title, "I would not now use this word to describe the experience which is central to this book. I would not, indeed, use it to describe anything, for I now believe it to be a word of such varying senses that it has become useless and should be banished from our vocabulary" (5). This was written in the preface to the third edition about 1943, and even then, defining Romanticism was a challenge. Oddly, after stating that the word is useless, Lewis, in his characteristic clarity, goes on to define "romantic" by laying down seven points. Distinguished from love stories, romantic can mean: 1) stories about dangerous adventure, 2) the marvelous and the fantastic, much in the sense that G.K. Chesterton thinks of the romantic and George MacDonald practices it, 3) "titanic characters," ie, larger than life artistic representations both visually and emotionally, 4) the macabre, 5) egoism and subjectivism, 6) "Every revolt against existing civilization and conventions," and last, 7) "Sensibility to natural objects" and Lewis mentions *The Prelude* here, as well as Goethe (5-6). Lewis follows this by pointing out that what he meant by Romanticism was simply his already well-known experience of joy and *Sehnsucht*. Once again, whatever else we may say of Lewis's Romanticism, this is central to it all. Of the list, numbers one through four correspond with our definition given in the preface and the various types of imaginative literature. Number five is debatable and mostly concerns Lord Byron, a poet that Lewis disliked. Number six corresponds with the Romantic sense of the intrinsic value of the common man. Not all revolts are romantic. Revolts of the common people against a despot are. And number seven corresponds with the Romantic idea of the intrinsic value of nature as a transcendental and spiritual force. Lewis goes on to say that by Romanticism, in this particular book, he means joy and the quest for *Sehnsucht*. This is a vital point in understanding the Romantic side of Lewis. Whatever other imagery or ideas he absorbs from the Romantics, joy is the central thing to him. And to define what joy is and what joy isn't, is vital to him. Thus Lewis will attack Romantic ideas with great energy if they are portrayed as a "first thing."

Lewis's protagonist, John, finds his childhood bewildering and discouraging, unable to understand the dual nature of the reverence and contempt that the inhabitants of Puritania hold for "The Landlord." He has a vision of an island, which Lewis's notes at the top of the page identify with joy. While journeying to find this island, he encounters the "brown girls," which represent lust, and for a time he mistakes his sexual drive for his desire for the island. Later on, when John is journeying along the main road to find the island in the company of Vertue, who symbolizes his conscience, he encounters Media Halfways, a beautiful young woman who convinces John to go with her south of the road. She takes him to her home where he meets Mr. Halfways. Lewis's notes on the top of the page read, "'Romantic' poetry professes to give what hitherto he has only desired" (42). Mr. Halfways therefore symbolizes Romantic poetry and the whole Romantic sensibility. When John mentions that he doesn't believe in the Landlord, Mr. Halfways says, "What the imagination seizes as beauty must be truth" (43). John believes himself to be in love with Media and that she is what he wants when he wants the island. Mr. Halfways sings songs that evoke the island and John wants them again and again until the illusion is shattered. John ultimately moves on.

Read in isolation, the scene as allegory appears to be a rather harsh condemnation of Romanticism by Lewis. And this is typical of Lewis's reaction to the whole issue of Romanticism and joy. As we discussed in the first chapter, for Lewis it is critical that "second things" not be mistaken for "first things." Lewis, as with his severe criticism of Wordsworth, energetically works to make sure his readers understand that no Romanticism, or Romantic poetry can ever become a viable substitute for God. They may evoke but that is the full extent of their power. Lewis wants no one to mistake joy, lust or anything for what the human soul really longs for, the living God.

Much further along in the story John is staying with a hermit in a cave that Lewis's top of the page gloss identifies as "History." Speaking with History, John learns perspective about his past experiences. John recounts how the "Clevers" abused Mr. Halfways, the symbol of Romantic poetry. History replies:

> Poor Halfways! They treat him very unfairly—as if he were anything more than the local representative of a thing as widespread and as necessary (though, withal, as dangerous) as the sky! Not a bard representative, either, if you take his songs in your stride and use them as they are meant to be used: of course people who go to him in cold blood to get as much pleasure as they can, and therefore hear the same song over and over again, have only themselves to thank if they wake in the arms of Media. (151)

Here again, Lewis, speaking through his allegorical character, explains his apparent ambivalence to Romanticism: use it right and it's wonderful. Mistake it for a "first thing," for faith itself, for ultimate meaning, and you will be misled. All of Lewis's apparent criticisms of Romanticism must be seen in this light.

What is certain is that *Till We Have Faces* is a darker book in terms of imagery from the Narnia chronicles or even the Ransom trilogy. Great sections of it are scenes in urban Glome or in the dark stone passages of Glome's royal palace. There is transcendence, but it is presented in darkness first. The principal goddess of Glome is Ungit, a fertility goddess like the Greek Aphrodite. Ungit's temple is "dark, holy and horrible" (125). The god of the mountain that Psyche is sacrificed to is the "Shadowbrute." The darkness is deep because the darkness is in the mind and the heart of the narrator, Orual. She is possessive and jealous of her beautiful little sister, Psyche, who is sacrificed to the Shadowbrute, and we don't see the imagery of light and greenness and glory that we've become so accustomed to seeing in Lewis's fantasies until we come into contact with the gods themselves. This happens when Orual and her father's chief guard, Bardia, go out on the mountain to look for Psyche's remains to bury them. First they experience such a level of natural beauty, that Orual almost has a change of heart.

> We now went for a long time over grass, gently but steadily upward, making for a ridge so high and so near that the true Mountain was out of sight. When we topped it, and stood for a while to let the horse breathe, everything was changed. And my struggle began.
> We had come into the sunlight now, too bright to look into, and warm (I threw back my cloak). Heavy dew made the grass jewel-bright. The Mountain, far greater yet also far further off than I expected, seen with the sun hanging a hand-breadth above its topmost crags, did not look like a solid thing. Between us and it was a vast tumble of valley and hill, woods

and cliffs, and more little lakes than I could count. To left and right, and behind us, the whole coloured world with all its hills was heaped up and up to the sky, with, far away, a gleam of what we call the sea. . . . There was a lark singing; but for that, huge and ancient stillness.

And my struggle was this. You may well believe that I had set out sad enough; I came on a sad errand. Now, flung at me like frolic or insolence, there came as if it were a voice—no words—but if you made it into words it would be, "Why should your heart not dance?" It's the measure of my folly that my heart almost answered, "Why not?"(95-6)

Orual is choked with possessive love and jealously which she will only lose at the end of the story in a vision and near death. But in this short scene she almost repents at the bright beauty. The description is similar in tone and imagery to scenes we quoted earlier from the Narnia stories and *The Great Divorce*. This is a glimpse of Heaven and even in her dark jealousy, Orual has a moment of joy. Shortly after this scene she finds Psyche in the god's wood, living in an invisible house of the god as his wife. The description of the wood there is as dark, cold and chilling as this description quoted above is bright and joyful. Lewis well understands not only is nature a sacrament, but that all the words and thought of the divine can be transmitted through it. In the scene above, nature is reflecting the divine beauty. In the scene shortly after with Psyche at the god's house, nature is reflecting not only Orual's anger and possessive passion, but the jealousy of the divine, to use the Old Testament term; God will not surrender the ones he loves.

Upon hearing how Psyche was rescued by the god, the West Wind, Orual exclaims, "Psyche, are you sure this happened? You must have been dreaming!" to which Psyche replies, "And if it was a dream, Sister, how do you think I came here? It's more likely everything that happened to me before this was a dream" (TWHF 112). Later on, Orual does see the palace on her second trip, but refuses to believe it and loses the ability to see it (132-4). Orual denies the perception of her imagination. When Psyche obeys Orual and looks upon her husband, the consequences include an electrical storm and rocks crashing from the cliffs. Nature reflects the anger of the god. Plus, Orual clearly hears the voice of the god and sees him plainly when he casts Psyche out and judges Orual, so that she cannot deny the perception of her imagination (170-4).

As Lewis's pattern is to heighten his natural descriptions in the presence of gods, and Orual thereafter goes through a long slog of years alone, the book veers away from too many more descriptions like the one quoted above. This sets it apart in imagery and tone from his other fictions, so that though it is a book about the imagination, in some ways it reflects a darker Romanticism, one that focuses on the darker half of human nature. The notable exception is the scene late in the book where Orual finds a temple to the new goddess, Istra, whom she recognizes to be Psyche. This shock to her complacent life comes as the other did, after a description of an autumn day, symbolic as Orual at this point is quite old and in the autumn of her life. Here, as in elsewhere in Lewis's fiction, a moment of divine epiphany, of self-knowledge, is prefaced by the sensory lushness of the natural world.

> It was the calmest day—pure autumn—very hot, yet the sunlight on the stubble looked aged and gentle, not fierce like summer heats. You would think the year was resting, its work done. . . . The hot spring . . . was only food for stupid wonder. When we had seen it we went further down the warm, green valley in which it rose and found a good camping place between a stream and a wood. . . . I went a little way into the wood and sat there in the coolness. Before long I heard the ringing of a temple bell . . . from somewhere behind me. Thinking it would be pleasant to walk a little after so many hours on horseback, I rose and went slowly through the trees to find the temple . . . . (240)

There in the temple, Orual is confronted by a version of the story of Psyche which blames her for Psyche's troubles. This jolt, coming as confrontations with the divine do in Lewis's fiction, at a scene of natural beauty, sends Orual back to Glome to begin writing her complaint against the gods. Orual then has a series of visions in which she is confronted by her dead father and the Fox and sees that she has been carrying Psyche's pain as Psyche does the tasks of her penance. In the final scene, Psyche's last task is to bring a cask of beauty to Orual, who recognizes that she has become like Ungit, swollen on the lives of others that she has consumed. Though the imagery is dark and cave-like here, Orual meets with the divine shortly before her own death, and finds that the god's words, "you too shall be Psyche" have come to mean that she has become beautiful. Thus in these final passages of Lewis's fiction, the protagonist achieves beauty in a vision and the Romantic side of Lewis's nature has the final word in fiction.

Chapter Eight

Lewis as Child Critic

The Child is Father of the Man;
And I could wish my days to be
Bound each to each by natural piety.
—From the "Immortality Ode" by William Wordsworth

There have been several worthy studies of Lewis's criticism, notably by Bruce Edwards and Peter Schakel. The most useful critique I've found was in my co-author, Donald Williams' *Mere Humanity* in Appendix A. But I wish to focus here on the Romantic element in Lewis's critical outlook, and not on the entire scope of his critical legacy as these critics have already done.

In order to understand Lewis as critic, it would be useful to look at the era in which he taught and wrote. Lewis entered the literary world right after the First World War, at the high tide of Modernism. Realism had been a literary force for nearly sixty years. Critics like F.R. Leavis were attempting to define literature in light of the ascendant Modernist sensibilities. In the spirit of Matthew Arnold several decades before, literature became a subject at the universities and writing that did not meet high critical standards, that was "popular," was considered bad art. Such literature, it was assumed, interested only those of low artistic standards, whom Arnold had labeled "philistines." As the study of literature began to ape the study of the sciences, the language of criticism became more specialized and loaded with jargon, so that just to read criticism required advanced study. Literature that was not realistic and did not have existential or naturalistic undertones, was not considered "serious." Most important, Modernism by its very definition rejects Victorian and Romantic values and attitudes.

Into this Modern post-war literary scene C.S. Lewis emerges as an author but also as a critic. Lewis himself wrote a significant amount of criticism, mostly in his field of Medieval and Renaissance literature. He wrote the volume in the *Oxford History of English Literature* in that very area. Unlike much literary criticism, his is a pleasure to read and doesn't require a dictionary of philosophical terms at hand for the average person to read it. The most severe complaint I have ever heard lodged against Lewis's criticism is that it tends to make the work under discussion sound more interesting than it actually is, and that there is more pleasure in reading Lewis's discussion than there is in reading the original work. His *Experiment in Criticism* was ground-breaking, but it hardly made a stir at the time of its publishing. Yet it had its genesis in earlier essays, later collected by Walter Hooper in *C.S. Lewis: On Stories and Other Essays on Literature,* which we will examine in depth.

Perhaps the key to understanding Lewis as a Romantic critic is in an essay "On Three Ways of Writing for Children" which dates to a talk given to the Library Association in 1952. Toward the end of the essay, Lewis writes:

> Once in a hotel dining-room I said, rather too loudly, 'I loathe prunes.' 'So do I,' came an unexpected six-year-old voice from another table. Sympathy was instantaneous. Neither of us thought it funny. We both knew that prunes were far too nasty to be funny. That is the proper meeting between man and child as independent personalities. (OS 42)

And though Lewis here is talking about how a writer of children's literature should avoid adult condescension and properly write for children, this is also how Lewis approaches a text as a critic. That is, Lewis criticizes literature from the point of view of a child. Of course, Lewis does not approach a text with the limited knowledge and experience of a child, but Lewis criticizes a text with an understanding that the principal reason for reading is for pleasure, that the principal reason for writing is communication without condescension and that the reader, like a child, is best addressed by any writer, whether or not he or she is a critic, with simple dignity. As we see in his dialog across restaurant tables with a six-year-old, Lewis talks on 'eye level' with the child; so does he talk on 'eye level' with his reader. There is no sense that only the philosophically sophisticated, the non-Philistines, are capable of understanding a text. There is no elitism in Lewis. Simple truth, as could be grasped at almost any age by anyone of reasonable intelligence, is sufficient. Books are not written solely for the elite, but for readers across the spectrum of humanity. Therefore, Lewis values a text not as vehicle for selling an existential or any other philosophical agenda, and thus he does not limit himself to any agenda such as Realism. It could be argued that his work is imbued with his Christian faith, but even here, Lewis never browbeats the reader or condescends. The reader is free to accept or reject without fear that Lewis will denigrate that reader's intelligence for not having conformed.

Lewis is not concerned whether a given piece of literature is "serious." There is no more virtue in literature for seriousness than there is for comedy. Both modes are options, neither having more or less merit except as in how well the author has composed them. There is no vital and moral superiority for seriousness in a work of fiction, drama or poetry. Also, Lewis is an historical critic because he believes that every age has its own characteristic insights and errors, and that you cannot understand a work unless you understand the context in which it was created. And last, Lewis defines the word "literary" to apply to any sort of reading or story that compels the reader to return and find pleasure on subsequent re-readings. Thus Lewis rejects any sort of pretension that literature might constitute a substitute for religion or philosophy, as a mode of finding the meaning of existence or that existence perhaps has no meaning. Even his Christian world view, unless the work is specifically apologetic, is always in the background. Many people have loved his Narnia tales without making any connection between them and the Christian faith. Literature is first and foremost a mode of pleasure and only second, a mode of widening one's vision of the world.

Lewis did not learn this approach at the knee of any great critic or in any particular school. Lewis learned it as a boy who had a house full of books and a tremendous amount of spare time in which to read them. In his autobiography he writes,

> I am a product of long corridors, empty sunlit rooms, upstairs indoor silences, attics explored in solitude, distant noises of gurgling cisterns and pipes, and the noise of wind under the tiles. Also, of endless books. . . . Nothing was forbidden me. In the seemingly endless rainy afternoons I took volume after volume from the shelves. I had always the same certainty of finding a book that was new to me as a man who walks into a field has of finding a new blade of grass. (SBJ 10)

It is almost impossible to overstate the importance of this experience as a boy with a book in a lonely attic on the shaping of Lewis as writer and critic. In a very real sense, he never ceased to be the boy in the attic, the boy who picked books off his father's crowded shelves. The child truly is father to the man, or more specifically, the child in the attic is the father to the critic and professor of Medieval and Renaissance Literature at Cambridge. Elsewhere in his autobiography, he admits to a principle about the reading of poetry that extends to all his reading: "There was a humility in me (as a reader) at that time which I shall never recapture. Some poems

I could not enjoy as well as others. It never occurred to me that these might be the inferior ones" (SBJ 163). And although he admittedly grows up to recognize good from bad here, he recognizes them by his own taste. He does not consult the critical consensus. Of course, such a thing is not remarkable for a boy, but the fact is, Lewis the man never does relegate his gut reactions to a secondary place in deference to the critical climate of his age. Lewis the author of the *Oxford History of English Literature* has recourse to the same source for his critical stance. Elsewhere he writes, "Never in my life had I read a work of fiction, poetry, or criticism in my own language except because, after trying the first few pages, I liked the taste of it" (SBJ 102-3). And in speaking of the difference between childhood and boyhood, he makes the wider observation, "My childhood is at unity with the rest of my life" (SBJ 71-2). Indeed, he writes of his early tastes in books, including the, ". . . E[dith] Nesbitt trilogy, *Five Children and It, The Phoenix and the Wishing Carpet,* and *The Amulet.* The last did most for me. It first opened my eyes to antiquity, the 'dark backward and abysm of time.' I can still reread it with delight" (SBJ 14). Lewis is writing this passage in his mid fifties and anyone familiar with his Narnia books for children will know the "dark backward and abysm of time" in passages in *The Silver Chair* and *The Magician's Nephew.* And we can readily believe that Lewis the middle-aged Professor of Medieval and Renaissance Literature at Cambridge was not above sitting down and pleasurably re-reading Edith Nesbitt's *The Amulet.*

In his 1947 essay "On Stories," Lewis lays out many of the positions that he took as a critic. At the start of the essay, he defines his primary taste for reading to be enjoying all the detail and texture of the imaginary world that he's entering. This is part of Lewis's Romanticism that he sees with a child's eyes the adult world and comprehends meaning with the imagination. He addresses this tendency to realism, that dismisses imaginative literature as childish.

> It is usual to speak in a playfully apologetic tone about one's adult enjoyment of what are called 'children's books'. I think the convention a silly one. No book is worth reading at the age of ten which is not equally (and often far more) worth reading at the age of fifty—except, of course, books of information. The only imaginative works we ought to grow out of are those which it would have been better not to have read at all. A mature palate will probably not much care for *crème de menthe*: but it ought still to enjoy bread and butter and honey. (OS 14)

This distinction Lewis makes in the essay between those who read to enter imaginary worlds and those who read for mere suspense develops for the first time into Lewis's most important, and indeed the only significantly divisive critical distinction Lewis makes. This distinction, considered and expanded becomes *An Experiment in Criticism* a little over a decade later. Lewis defines a new way to use the words "literary" and "unliterary" which I will explore in the section on *An Experiment in Criticism*. I will merely say here that they turn entirely on the concept of reading primarily being a mode of pleasure. Lewis, the child reading in an empty attic, finds the chief use of literature to be mental travel into imaginary worlds.

In "On Three Ways of Writing for Children," Lewis puts forward a principle, that,

> Where the children's story is simply the right form for what the author has to say, then of course readers who want to hear that will read the story or re-read it, at any age. I never met *The Wind in the Willows* or the [Edith Nesbitt's] Bastable books till I was in my late twenties, and I do not think I have enjoyed them any the less on that account. I am almost inclined to set it up as a canon that a children's story which is enjoyed only by children is a bad children's story. The good ones last. A waltz which you can like only when you are waltzing is a bad waltz. (OS 33)

Lewis continues with a defense of his attitude towards literature, the concept of "adult" and "childish" and of "Fairy Tales," which is eloquent and far too long to quote here. I will summarize: Lewis objects for three reasons to using the word "adult" to categorize books. First, he argues that, "critics who treat *adult* as a term of approval, instead of a merely descriptive term, cannot be adults themselves" (OS 34). The reason is that only children and adolescents worry about appearing adult and to do so betrays a lack of maturity. "When I was ten," he writes, " I read fairy tales in secret and would have been ashamed if I had been found doing so. Now that I am fifty, I read them openly" (OS 34).

Second, Lewis accuses the modern view of arrested development because of an erroneous view of growth. Rejection of the past is not growth; rather the addition of new developments to old goods is. These first two reasons, though Lewis does not say so in the text, constitute one of the clearest reasons why Lewis the critic had little to no sympathy with Modernism, whose chief trait was the rejection of the Victorian and pre-Victorian past. Indeed, from his argument here, it is clear that Lewis views older literary periods as a kind of literary childhood in Western Culture and Modernism and Postmodernism as its rocky and obnoxious adolescence. Dare we hope that Western Culture's young adulthood might be less dark and chaotic? That remains to be seen. Lewis clearly knew himself to be separate from the Modern spirit, as he so eloquently explained in his inaugural address at Cambridge University.

Lewis's third defense is to reiterate JRR Tolkien's point that the assigning of fairy tales and fantastic literature to the nursery is merely a matter of literary fashion. He also briefly summarizes Jung's theory of archetypes, but then he offers his own theory which is a major piece of his own critical outlook:

> I would venture to add to this my own theory, not indeed of the Kind [ie fairy tales] as a whole, but of one feature to it: I mean, the presence of beings other than human which yet behave, in varying degrees, humanly: the giants and dwarfs and talking beasts. I believe these to be at least (for they have many other sources of power and beauty) an admirable hieroglyphic which conveys psychology, types of character, more briefly than novelistic presentation and to readers whom novelistic presentation could not yet reach. Consider Mr Badger in *The Wind and the Willows*— that extraordinary amalgam of high rank, coarse manners, gruffness, shyness, and goodness. The child who has once met Mr Badger has ever afterwards, in its bones, a knowledge of humanity and of English social history which it could not get in any other way. (OS 36)

This is a powerful counter-attack to the base assumption of Realism, denying that strictly realistic representations are required for literature to portray the truths of existence. This assumption that underlies Realism, underlies the assumptions of Naturalism as well. Emile Zola's strictures that the novel should be a kind of scientific experiment with realistic, scientifically verifiable and material phenomena is an unnecessary inhibition on literary art to Lewis. This, of course, is what is really meant by "serious," this pseudo-scientific and materialistic set of assumptions underlying the approach to a work of literature. The implication that fantasy and other non-realistic forms of writing are somehow childish, as we clearly see, is an idea Lewis firmly rejects. For Lewis, as perhaps for Jung, fantasy is the psychological literature before there was psychology. The fantastic portrays psychological and spiritual realities that can't be metered or measured or poked with a stick. Nor does Lewis concede to Naturalism the unprovable assumption that only the material world exists. Nature is not a sum total of matter and energy but rather a sign of eternity and here Lewis is Romantic in his outlook. It is also an illustration of Lewis's concept of the imagination as primarily metaphor. Thus imagination conveys meaning through the power of metaphor.

These concepts illuminate Lewis as critic. His works include: *The Allegory of Love, Oxford History of English Literature in the Sixteenth Century Excluding Drama, A Preface to 'Paradise Lost', Spenser's Images of Life, Medieval and Renaissance Literature, The Discarded Image, Studies in Words,* and also *Selected Literary Essays.* The voice in the criticism is confident and the matter is historical context. Lewis never imposes a twentieth century view on the past. He is an historical critic and his object is to promote clarity and understanding. In the opening of *A Preface to 'Paradise Lost',* he lays out his principle for that book, which in fact is his approach to all criticism. "The first qualification for judging any piece of workmanship from a corkscrew to a cathedral is to know what it is—what it was intended to do and how it is meant to be used" (PPL 1). This precludes looking at a piece of literature and imposing a Freudian or Feminist or for that matter, any system of thought that is foreign to the historical world in which the work of literature was created. In his essay "On the Reading of Old Books," Lewis enlarges on this principle.

> Every age has its own outlook. It is specially good at seeing certain truths and specially liable to make certain mistakes. We all, therefore, need the books that will correct the characteristic mistakes of our own period. And that means the old books. . . . The only palliative is to keep the clean sea breeze of the centuries blowing through our minds . . . . (GID 202)

Lewis is in fact more of an historicist than the current generation of new historicists. For a contemporary historicist is just as likely to feel that the present age has evolved and that though historical context is important, our present age is a vast improvement over the past in all things, not just in medicine and technology. Lewis is not impressed with the idea that culture, humanity evolves for the better. This was a point of disagreement between him and Barfield. For him, human nature is pretty even across the ages and human literature reflects that consistency. Therefore no age has the corner on wisdom, virtue or vice.

This opposition to the idea that humanity is evolving, and that culture is evolving, is central to Lewis's critical stance. In his essay "The Funeral of a Great Myth," Lewis takes on what he calls "Evolutionism." He is careful to distinguish between this and Darwin's theory, as Lewis does not hold to a literal reading of the opening chapters of Genesis. According to Lewis, the myth is the idea that everything is evolving upward, especially humanity. First there is,

> Man. . . . He thrives. . . . He becomes Cave Man . . . a brute yet somehow able to invent art, pottery, language, weapons, cookery and nearly everything else. . . . In his next act he becomes true Man. He learns to master Nature. Science arises and dissipates the superstitions of his infancy. More and more he becomes the controller of his own fate. . . . . we follow our hero on into the future. . . . A race of demi-gods now rule the

planet. . . . Eugenics have made certain that only demi-gods will now be born: psycho-analysis that none of them shall lose or smirch his divinity: economics that they shall have to hand all that demi-gods require. Man has ascended his throne. (87-8)

Though Lewis here enjoys mocking this myth, it is a powerful one and prevalent in our post-Darwinian Western Culture. In the nihilistic and existential world-view that underlies much of twentieth century literature, science is seen to have dispensed with religion and psycho-analysis to have dispensed with traditional morality. The whole energy of Modernism was bent on rejecting these traditions. What takes their place is this vague faith that humanity now aided by science will solve its own problems, that all mental processes are merely chemistry and therefore reparable by drugs. Lewis opposes all this. Of course this faith in Evolutionism is not universal among writers with a naturalistic or existential world view. As often as not, they hold out no hope whatsoever. But with the Modernist rejection of traditional faith, faith in the supposed evolution of humanity in a material universe is one of the few options.

Of course, this is not to say that Lewis in writing fantasy is escaping reality, the gritty realities that are often portrayed in so-called "serious" fiction of the twentieth century. But Lewis approaches these issues, whether in his own form of reverse-psychological fiction as in the *Screwtape Letters*, the exploration of the psyche in *Till We Have Faces*, or in more direct essay form in *Mere Christianity* and other non-fiction from a standpoint that does not assume a meaningless universe and does not toss traditional values on the dust heap of history before addressing a matter.

Ironically, Lewis became, for lack of a better term, an anti-Modernist, though the term he used for himself was not anti-Modern but rather a dinosaur, in his inaugural address. And though in that address he characterized himself as one of the last of a vanishing breed, the resurgent Romanticism of the fantasy and science fiction movement that he and Tolkien prominently led in mid-century constituted a full fledged counter movement in literature.

If there is any good cause why Lewis should be seen as a major voice in criticism in the twentieth century, it is his contribution in his little 1961 book, *An Experiment in Criticism*. Lewis wrote the book, one of his last, in response to the whole critical atmosphere surrounding FR Leavis' presence at Cambridge. Leavis' book *The Great Tradition* proposed to rate literary works by their originality, thus condemning the novels of George Eliot to non-entity because Jane Austen had already done something like them, a kind of literary Evolutionism where each development of a new type renders all others irrelevant, and to evolve is the only road to quality in literature. At the time, Leavis had a high reputation and many followers, having become somewhat of a literary pope reigning in Cambridge. Lewis proposes an entirely different way of looking at and evaluating the worth of books that sent a torpedo into Leavis' whole approach, rendering it, if one took Lewis seriously, as entirely irrelevant. I cannot find any record of formal debates between the two Cambridge professors, though I have heard rumor that Leavis was more than a little put out by Lewis's book and the epithet of "literary Puritan" being applied to him and his movement. No doubt the pubs and commons rooms in Cambridge buzzed for some time. But ultimately, perhaps because Lewis's health was failing, the clash of these two titans never came off.

Lewis's proposal is devastatingly simple. What if instead of rating books we rate the way they are read. What if instead of evaluating books we evaluate readers. Lewis makes a distinction between the literary and unliterary reader, but not in any sense that Matthew Arnold would recognize. For Lewis, the literary reader is one who savors books, and more specifically, re-reads books and immerses himself or herself in the texture of the imaginary world that he or she enters through its pages. The unliterary reader on the other hand, uses books. They never re-read and either read for the simple suspense of the plot or because they are a professional teacher or critic who reads because it is a professional requirement. Having made this distinction, Lewis defines good literature as books that invite a literary reading. This explodes all the distinctions made by Arnold or Leavis or other critics in their mold. Furthermore, unlike Arnold with his scorn of Philistines, Lewis is careful to state that there is no moral virtue or vice attached to being literary or unliterary: it is simply a matter of art, not profound philosophy or moral purity.

Lewis refuses to attach a high virtue to "serious" literature. In the *Experiment*, Lewis condemns critics who make a labor of what should be a joy, that read a book because it is the critical sensation of the moment. He writes:

> This laborious sort of misreading is perhaps especially prevalent in our own age. One sad result of making English Literature a 'subject' at schools and universities is that the reading of great authors is, from early years, stamped upon the minds of conscientious and submissive young people as something meritorious. When the young person in question is an agnostic whose ancestors were Puritans, you get a regrettable state of mind. The Puritan conscience works on without the Puritan theology—like millstones grinding nothing; like digestive juices working on an empty stomach and producing ulcers. The unhappy youth applies to literature all the scruples, the rigorism, the self-examination, the distrust of pleasure, which he forebears applied to the spiritual life; and perhaps soon all the intolerance

and self-righteousness. The doctrine of Dr I. A. Richards in which the correct reading of good poetry has a veritable therapeutic value confirms him in this attitude. The Muses assume the role of the Eumenides. A young woman most penitently confessed to a friend of mine that an unholy desire to read the woman's magazines was her besetting 'temptation'.

It is the existence of these literary Puritans that has deterred me from applying the word *serious* to the right sort of readers and reading.   It suggests itself at first as just the word we want. But it is fatally equivocal. . . . . Now a true reader reads every work seriously in the sense that he reads it whole-heartedly, makes himself receptive as he can. But for that very reason he cannot possibly read every work solemnly or gravely. For he will read 'in the same spirit that the author writ'. What is meant lightly he will take lightly; what is meant gravely, gravely. . . .

This is where the literary Puritans may fail most lamentably. They are too serious as men to be seriously receptive as readers. I have listened to an undergraduate's paper on Jane Austen from which, if I had not read them, I should have never discovered that there was the least hint of comedy in her novels. After a lecture of my own I have been accompanied from Mill Lane to Magdalene by a young man protesting real anguish and horror against my wounding, my vulgar, my irrelevant, suggestion that *The Miller's Tale* was written to make people laugh. And I have heard of another who finds *Twelfth Night* a penetrating study of the individual's relation to society. . . . .   Solemn men, but not serious readers; they have not fairly and squarely laid their minds open, without preconception, to the works they read. (EC 10-12)

To read a story for pleasure is the primary goal of both the child and the literary reader, who reads a work with a child's simple sense of joy and a child's tendency to relish re-reading of a favorite work. The unliterary use a text wrongly. Those who make a moral act of reading are literary Puritans, who destroy the pleasure of reading to make it a sort of sour religion. Seriousness is not a virtue and is a concept misunderstood, where literature is mistaken for religion. And finally, a text should be read for what it was intended to be: a comedy is a comedy and not a sociological study on stage.

Lewis addresses the insistence on realism in literature in the seventh chapter of the *Experiment*. He makes distinction between realism of presentation, that is in giving lots of specific imagery in a passage of fiction, and realism of content, wherein any elements of fantasy are excluded. Lewis's own words on this in the *Experiment* are unequivocal.

In this age it is important to remind ourselves that all four ways of writing [various types of realism] are good and masterpieces can be produced in any of them. The dominant taste at present demands realism of content.

> The great achievements of the nineteenth-century novel have trained us to appreciate and to expect it. But we should be making a disastrous mistake and creating one more false classification of books and readers if we erected this natural and historically conditioned preference into a principle. There is some danger of this. No one that I know of has indeed laid down in so many words that a fiction cannot be fit for adult and civilised reading unless it represents life as we have all found it to be, or probably shall find it to be, in experience. But some such assumption seems to lurk tacitly in the background of much criticism and literary discussion. We feel it in the widespread neglect or disparagement of the romantic, the idyllic, and the fantastic, and the readiness to stigmatise instances of these as 'escapism'. (EIC 60)

Lewis goes on to prove in detail that no such scruple of realism can be maintained, that fiction will always defy a clean distinction or definition. He argues that the point of the story is not to portray real life, a notion taken from Zola and the Naturalists, but to ask, "Suppose this happened, how interesting, how moving the consequences would be!" (EIC 66). He adds,

> The effort to force such stories into a radically realistic theory of literature seems to me perverse. . . . The demand that all literature should have realism of content cannot be maintained. Most of the great literature so far produced in the world has not. But there is a quite different demand which we can properly make; not that all books should be realistic in content, but that every book should have as much of this realism as it pretends to have." (EIC 66-7)

It is hard to understate the devastating implications of these ideas on the present state of English criticism. If they were taken seriously, the whole discipline would have to be rethought. Much of what passes today for legitimate critical activity would have to be discarded. Is it any surprise that English academia has by and large ignored *An Experiment in Criticism?* To attend to its principles would put a lot of people out of work.

There is a temptation here to label Lewis an anachronism, and he was a self-proclaimed "dinosaur." But I think that was an unjust characterization. For if he is a dinosaur, he is no slow Brachiosaurus dragging himself into the scene, but rather he is a raptor, who has taken a clean chunk out of the flanks of modern English criticism and they have pretended for the last forty-five years that it never happened. He is a Romantic critic resurgent in the Modern age. He is an advocate for reading as an art form whose primary purpose is to bring pleasure. If it does have a secondary purpose, it might be illumination, but not in the laden philosophical and sociological sense required by literary Puritans. Lewis concludes his *Experiment* by saying:

> But in reading great literature I become a thousand men and yet remain myself. Like the night sky in the Greek poem, I see with myriad eyes, but it is still I who see. Here, as in worship, in love, in moral action, and in knowing, I transcend myself; and am never more myself than when I do. (EC 141)

We read for pleasure. We gain perspective. Those of us who love books and don't just use them are all like children in a book-filled attic on a rainy day. This is enough. Literature is not religion; it is merely art. As Lewis noted in passing in his essay, "First and Second Things,"

> Until quite modern times . . . nobody ever suggested that literature and the arts were an end in themselves. They 'belonged to the ornamental part of life', they provided 'innocent diversion'; or else they 'refined our manners' or 'incited us to virtue' or glorified the gods. . . . It was only in the nineteenth century that we became aware of the full dignity of art. We began to 'take it seriously' . . . . But the result seems to have been a dislocation of the aesthetic life in which little is left for us but high-minded works which fewer and fewer people want to read or hear or see, and 'popular' works of which those who make them and those who enjoy them are half ashamed. (GID 279-280)

To elevate art to almost a religious state is to lose it, to divide it between the self-proclaimed elite and the masses, to introduce a moral dimension where none really exists. Lewis's critical stance in the *Experiment* may now be one iceberg floating alone, almost entirely ignored in the sea of human thought. But it is enough to sink the Titanic of English criticism as it is now practiced. Only future generations will judge.

CONCLUSION

LEAVIS, LEWIS, AND POSTMODERNISM

In arguing for the Romantic side of Lewis, I am arguing for a context by which we may consider him more than just a "religious writer." If Lewis deserves a significant place in English literature, perhaps beside his fellow genius Coleridge, it is because he manages to marry these two polar opposites, reason and romance. In so doing he has brought a balance and a staying power to the fleeting visions of Romanticism. And this alone should earn him a major place in the history of Western thought. His great work is to have defined across the body of his writing the right relation between reason on one hand and imagination and feeling on the other. His most succinct statement is from the essay "Bluspells and Flalansferes" where Lewis tells us that reason is the organ of truth and imagination the organ of meaning. What were take-one-or-the-other alternatives become two sides of the coin of truth, which we can hold in the palm of our hand. Reason and Romance have met and kissed in Lewis's philosophy, and the celebrant of the wedding is Christ Himself. And this perhaps is Lewis's great achievement.

Indeed, the unrealized conflict between C.S. Lewis and F.R. Leavis has significance far beyond a war of words between two members of the Cambridge faculty in the mid to late 50s. Both Lewis and Leavis were teaching at Oxford and Cambridge at a time when the profession of English teaching at the university level was relatively new. Rhetoric had long been taught, but the teaching of literature in English was a turn-of-the-century innovation and controversial. Lewis and Tolkien were involved in the debates at Oxford as to how much English literature should be taught. Throughout the 20s and 30s the Oxford faculty refused to teach any literature after the mid 1700s, because if was felt that anything newer would be too close and criticism would lack the necessary objectivity. Both Leavis and Lewis were critics and university literature teachers at a time when the profession of literary criticism in English was being defined. Thus, Leavis' *Great Tradition* came out at a critical moment. We wonder what might have happened had Lewis's *An Experiment in*

Criticism come out first. Leavis's book was published in 1948—Lewis's book was published in 1961. By the time Lewis weighed in, his response was a late reaction. By the time Lewis's book became known, Leavis was an established head of a faction. Other than the *Experiment*, Lewis refrained from public comment. In private, Lewis could be quite acid in his comments on Leavis. In a 1962 letter to J.B. Priestly, he writes:

> Leavis himself is something (in the long run) more fatal than a villain. He is a perfectly sincere, disinterested, fearless, ruthless fanatic. I am sure he would, if necessary, die for his critical principles: I am afraid he might also kill for them. Ultimately, a pathological type – unhappy, intense, mirthless. Incapable of conversation: dead silence or prolonged, passionate, and often irrelevant, monologue are his only two lines. And while he is in fact the head of the most powerful literary Establishment we have ever had since Boileau, he maddeningly regards himself as a solitary martyr with his back to the wall. (CLCSL3, 1372)

Lewis, on the other hand, was almost completely the opposite of these traits. Upon his arrival at Cambridge in 1955, Lewis described himself in his inaugural address as a dinosaur. He made it blindingly clear that he was not a Modernist. He stood by his Christian and Romantic principles in spite of the Leavis faction at Cambridge. Had he started sooner and had not been bucking the Modernist trends of the time, one wonders if he would have changed the nature of English literary criticism and English literature itself. But looking at the *Experiment in Criticism* and other texts which we have examined in this study, we see several principles that Lewis stands for against Modernism.

1) No era should presume to define itself. Objectivity requires distance.

2) Literature is not a religion, nor a substitute for one.

3) Literature should be read in the spirit it was written. Re-interpretation is vain and irrelevant.

4) Reading is a pleasure, not an exercise in philosophy, nor an imposition of the dominant philosophy of a given movement on common people.

5) When the common people, the readership, turn their backs on high-sounding, or bleak philosophies buried in literature, they are not philistines or fools. They just know what they enjoy reading.

6) To define something by saying it has no boundaries is to not define it. It is to identify that thing as an illusion.

Numbers 1 and 6 are especially pertinent to Postmodernism. As I wrote elsewhere (Prothero 2012, 3), Lewis refused to use the term "Renaissance," because he felt that it was a term by which Humanists optimistically defined themselves and lacked specificity and objectivity. (OHEL 55-56) And Postmodernists will define their movement as one that eschews all boundaries. In that article I argued that Postmodernism was a patch job of a definition that lumped together everything happening in the arts and thought after the second world war under one convenient name that was self-chosen. On the principles that he used to doubt the accuracy of the term "Renaissance," I argued that Lewis would no doubt have equally questioned the term "Postmodernism."

But there is one element in the Leavis versus Lewis debate that I believe actually does define and drive Postmodernism. Leavis argued that the primary way of judging quality in literature was the originality of its concept. I believe it is this same fixation on originality that actually does define Postmodernism. Thus, Postmodernism is the fixation with originality. In any case, we believe that the self-defined history of twentieth century literature needs to be re-examined.

Our own conclusion is that modern culture goes through cycles between expressions of the hyper-rational and the hyper-romantic and back again. As we defined it in a previous chapter, Romanticism is the perennial reaction to excessive rationalism. And we take the rise of science fiction and fantasy on one hand, and the rise of nature writing, on the other, both mainly after mid-century, to be a Romantic counter-movement that rose in reaction to the excessive and bleak rationalism behind existentialism and the nihilism that underlay it.

A more accurate reading of the century just completed would be that when the bleakness of Existentialism had run its natural course between the World Wars, the literate and the academic community mistakenly thought of the direction of literature as developing in a straight line and expected that development to continue and to evolve further in the same direction. They never believed that modern culture might take a pendulum swing back to forms of Romanticism. T.S. Eliot himself illustrates this pendulum motion if we consider the "Dead end of doubt" as expressed in "The Hollow Men" and "The Wasteland" and how they are followed by faith in "Ash Wednesday" and "The Four Quartets." But our culture does not evolve in a straight line. And the battle to force literary western culture to "evolve" is ultimately silly. Linear cultural evolution has failed. Instead, culture is doing what it has always done in books as it does in clothes— just wait long enough and yesterday's fashion will be hip again. Thus, the literary history of the twentieth century should be seen as two streams running parallel: first the Modernist, nihilistic stream, which is now mistaken for the mainstream, and then Romantic stream, running in parallel reaction.

This explains the odd phenomenon of the just completed century of the polarity between "serious literature" that is recommended by English professors and is often ignored by the reading public, and the so-called "genre fiction," of mystery, thrillers, fantasy, science fiction and other neo-romantic forms. The nineteenth century knew no such division between quality and popular literature.

In the meantime, Lewis is one of many Romantic writers of fantasy and science fiction emerging in the mid twentieth century. Romanticism resurrects itself in yet a new form, as it always seems to do. Lewis is the standard bearer of a form of Christian Romanticism, picking up the standard from Chesterton and MacDonald before him. And Lewis is a dissident voice in English criticism, defending the pleasure of reading and the primary reason for reading to be pleasure. He is a lone prophetic voice crying in the twentieth century wilderness. We do not believe it will always be so.

WORKS CITED OR CONSULTED

Batho, Edith Clara. 1933. *The Later Wordsworth*. New York: Macmillan.

Barfield, Owen. *Own Barfield on C.S. Lewis*. 1989. ed. George Tennyson. Middletown: Wesleyan University Press.

—. 1971. *What Coleridge Thought*. Middletown: Wesleyan University Press.

Brantley, Richard E. 1975. *Wordsworth's "Natural Methodism"*. New Haven: Yale University Press.

Carnell, Corbin Scott. 1974. *Bright Shadow of Reality: C. S. Lewis and the Feeling Intellect*. Grand Rapids: Eerdmans.

Chesterton, G.K. 2011. *The Collected Works: Volume 36; the London Illustrated News 1932-1934*. San Francisco: Ignatius.

—. 1955. *The Everlasting Man*. New York: Image.

—. 1959. *Oxthodoxy: The Romance of Faith*. New York: Image.

Coleridge, Samuel Taylor. 1949 *The Philosophical Lectures [1818-1819] Hitherto Unpublished*. London: Pilot Press.

C.S. Lewis Centenary Internet Newsletter. 16 July 2004 http://dnausers.d-n-a.net/cslewis/home.html.

Curtis, Jared. 1883. *Poems, In Two Volumes: and Other Poems*. The Cornell Wordsworth Series, Stephen Parrish, ed. Ithaca: Cornell University Press.

De Selincourt, Ernest. 1967. *Letters of William and Dorothy Wordsworth: the Early Years, 1787-1805*. Oxford: Oxford University Press.

—. 1967, 1969 *Letters of William and Dorothy Wordsworth: the Middle Years, 1806-1820*. Oxford: Oxford University Press.

—. 1967. *Letters of William and Dorothy Wordsworth: the Later Years, 1821-1853*. Oxford: Oxford University Press.

Downing, David. 2005. *Mysticism in C.S. Lewis: Into the Region of Awe*. Downers Grove: Intervarsity Press.

Dubay, Thomas, S. M. 1999. *The Evidential Power of Beauty*. San Francisco: Ignatius Press.

Easterlin, Nancy. 1996. *Wordsworth and the Question of "Romantic Religion"*. Lewisburg: Bucknell University Press.

Gill, Stephen. ed. 1984. *William Wordsworth: A Critical Edition of the Major Works*. Oxford: Oxford University Press.

—. 1989. *William Wordsworth: A Life*. Oxford: Oxford University Press.

—. 1967. "Wordsworth's 'Never Failing Principle of Joy'." *ELH* 34, no 2 (June): 208-224.

—. 1998. *Wordsworth and the Victorians.* Oxford: Oxford University Press,

Green, Roger Lancelyn Green and Walter Hooper. 1974. *C.S. Lewis: A Biography.* New York: Harcourt.

Gresham, Douglas. 1995."Memories of My Stepfather." St Andrew's Abbey, Valyermo. Talk given July 1995.

Griffin, William. 1986. *Clive Staples Lewis: A Dramatic Life.* San Francisco: Harper.

Hein, Rolland. 1993.*George MacDonald: Victorian Mythmaker.* Nashville: Star Song.

Hill, Alan G. 1984. *Letters of William Wordsworth: A New Selection.* Oxford: Clarendon Press.

Hipolito, Jane. 2007. "C. S. Lewis and Owen Barfield: Adversaries and Confidantes." *C.S. Lewis: Life, Works, and Legacy.* Vol 1. ed Bruce L. Edwards. Westport, Conn: Praeger,

Keats, John. 1970. *Poetical Works.* Oxford: Oxford University Press.

Kilby, Clyde S. 1964. *The Christian World of C. S. Lewis.* Grand Rapids: Eerdmans.

—. 1961. *Christianity and Aesthetics.* Chicago: Inter-Varsity Press.

Kreeft, Peter. 2008. "Lewis's Philosophy of Truth, Goodness, and Beauty." *C. S. Lewis as Philosopher: Truth, Goodness, and Beauty*, ed. David Baggett, Gary R. Habermas, and Jerry L. Walls. Downers Grove, Il.: InterVarsity Press: 32-36.

Kuhn, Daniel K. 1971. "The Joy of the Absolute: A Comparative Study of the Romantic Visions of William Wordsworth and C.S. Lewis." *Imagination and the Spirit.* Charles A. Huttar, ed. Grand Rapids: Eerdmans.

Leavis, F.R. 1963. *The Great Tradition.* New York: New York University Press.

Lewis, C.S. 1947. *The Abolition of Man, or Reflections on Education with Special Reference to the Teaching of English in the Upper Forms of Schools.* N.Y.: MacMillan.

—. 1936. *The Allegory of Love.* Oxford: Oxford University Press.

—. 2004. *The Collected Letters of C.S. Lewis.* Vol 1. ed Walter Hooper. San Francisco: Harpercollins.

—. 2004. *The Collected Letters of C.S. Lewis.* Vol 2. ed Walter Hooper. San Francisco: Harpercollins.

—. 2007. *The Collected Letters of C.S. Lewis.* Vol 3. ed Walter Hooper. San Francisco: Harpercollins.

—. 1967. *Christian Reflections.* ed Walter Hooper. Grand Rapids: Eerdmans.

—. 1966 (1982). *C.S. Lewis On Stories and Other Essays on Literature.* Walter Hooper, ed. New York: Harcourt.

—. 1964. *The Discarded Image.* Cambridge: Cambridge University Press,

—. 1967. *"De Futilitate." Christian Reflections*, ed. Walter Hooper. Grand Rapids: Eerdmans: 57-71.

—. 1954. *English Literature in the Sixteenth Century Excluding Drama.* Oxford: Clarendon Press.

—. 1961. *An Experiment in Criticism.* Cambridge: Cambridge University Press.

—. 1942. "First and Second Things." Orig. pub. as "Note on the Way," *Time and Tide* 23 (27 June): 519-20.

—. 1970. *God in the Dock: Essays on Theology and Ethics*, ed. Walter Hooper. Grand Rapids: Eerdmans: 278-81.

—. 1960. *The Four Loves.* N.Y.: Harcourt, Brace & World.

—. 1970. *God in the Dock: Essays on Theology and Ethics.* Grand Rapids: Eerdmans.

—. 1946. *The Great Divorce.* New York: Collier.

—. 1961. *A Grief Observed.* N.Y.: Seabury.

—. 1954. *The Horse and His Boy.* New York: Macmillan.

—. 1956. *The Last Battle.* New York: Macmillan,.

—. 1963. *Letters to Malcolm: Chiefly on Prayer.* N.Y.: Harcourt, Brace, Jovanovich.

—. 1950. *The Lion, the Witch and the Wardrobe.* New York: Macmillan.

—. 1955. *The Magician's Nephew.* New York: Macmillan.

—. 1947 *.Miracles: A Preliminary Study.* N.Y.: MacMillan.

—. 1960. *The Pilgrim's Regress: An Allegorical Apology for Christianity, Reason, and Romanticism.* London: Bless, 1933; rpt. Grand Rapids: Eerdmans

—. 1967. "The Poison of Subjectivism." *Religion in Life* 12 (Summer 1943); rpt. in *Christian Reflections*, ed. Walter Hooper. Grand Rapids: Eerdmans: 72-81.

—. 1961. *A Preface to Paradise Lost.* Oxford: Oxford University Press.

—. 1951. *.Prince Caspian.* New York: Macmillan.

—. 1969. *Selected Literary Essays.* Walter Hooper, ed. Cambridge: Cambridge University Press.

—. 1953. *The Silver Chair.* New York: Macmillan.

—. 1942. *The Screwtape Letters.* London: Collins.

—. 1967. *Spenser's Images of Life*. Alastair Fowler, ed. Cambridge: Cambridge University Press,

—. 1966. *Studies in Medieval and Renaissance Literature*. Cambridge: Cambridge University Press.

—. 1960. *Studies in Words*. Cambridge: Cambridge University Press.

—. 1955. *Surprised by Joy: The Shape of my Early Life*. N.Y.: Harcourt, Brace & World.

—. 1956. *Till We Have Faces*. New York: Harcourt.

—. 1952. *The Voyage of the Dawn Treader*. New York: Macmillan.

—. 1949. *The Weight of Glory and Other Addresses* (pub. in England under the title *Transposition and Other Addresses*). N.Y.: MacMillan,; rpt. Grand Rapids: Eerdmans, 1965.

MacDonald, George. 1995. *A Dish of Orts*. Reprint from original 1893 ed. Whitethorn: Johanessen.

—. 1893. *Sir Gibbie*. Boston: Lothman.

—. 1993. *The Princess and the Goblin*. Reprint from original 1872 ed. Whitethorn: Johanessen.

MacDonald, Greville. 1924. George MacDonald and His Wife. London: Allen and Unwin.

McGillis, Roderick. 1991. "Childhood and Growth: George MacDonald and William Wordsworth". *Romanticism and Children's Literature in the 19th Century*. James Holt McGavran, ed. Athens:University of Georgia Press.

—. 1992. *For the Childlike: George MacDonald's Fantasies for Children*. Lanham: Scarecrow Press.

—. 1978. Meilander, Gilbert. *The Taste for the Other: The Social and Ethical Thought of C. S. Lewis*. Grand Rapids: Eerdmans.

Moorman, Mary. 1957 (1965).*William Wordsworth: A Biography The Early Years 1770-1803*. Oxford: Clarendon Press.

—. 1965. *William Wordsworth: A Biography The Later Years 1803-1850*. Oxford: Clarendon P,

Noyes, Alfred, ed. 1956. *English Romantic Poetry and Prose*. N.Y.: Oxford University Press.

Patterson, Charles I. 1970. *The Daemonic in the Poetry of John Keats*. Chicago: The University of Illinois Press.

Polanyi, Michael. 1964. *Personal Knowledge: Towards a Post-Critical Philosophy*. N.Y.: Harper Torchbooks.

Prickett, Stephen. 1976. *Romanticism and Religion: The Tradition of Coleridge and Wordsworth in the Victorian Church*. Cambridge: Cambridge University Press.

Prothero, James. 1998. "Beauty." *The C. S. Lewis Reader's Encyclopedia*. Ed. Jeffrey D. Schultz and John G. West, Jr. Grand Rapids: Zondervan: 94.

—. 2012. "Lewis as Dissident Voice in the Post-Modern World." *The Lamp-Post*: Vol 34 No 3.

Reilly, R. J. 1971. *Romantic Religion: A Study of Barfield, Lewis, Williams and Tolkien*. Athens: University of Georgia Press.

Renwick, W. L. 1963. *.English Literature, 1789-1815*. Vol. IX of *The Oxford History of English Literature*. Oxford: Oxford University Press.

Robinson, Henry Crabb. 1938. *Henry Crabb Robinson on Books and their Writers*. Edith J Morley, ed. 3 vols. London: Dent.

Sayer, George. 1988. *Jack: C.S. Lewis and his Times*. New York: Harper.

Schakel, Peter J. 1984. *Reason and Imagination in C.S. Lewis: A Study of Till We Have Faces*. Grand Rapids: Eerdmans.

Ulmer, William A. 2001. *The Christian Wordsworth: 1798-1805*. Albany: State University of New York Press.

Veldman, Meredith. 1994. Fantasy, the Bomb and the Greening of Britain: Romantic Protest, 1945-1980. Cambridge University Press.

Von Balthasar, Hans Urs. 1982. *The Glory of the Lord: A Theological Aesthetics*, vol. 1: *Seeing the Form*. San Francisco: Ignatius Press.

Wasserman, Earl. 1964. "The Ode on a Grecian Urn." *Keats: A Collection of Critical Essays*, ed. Walter Jackson Bate. Englewood Cliffs, N.J.: Prentice Hall: 113-41.

Williams, Donald T. 2006. *Mere Humanity: G. K. Chesterton, C. S. Lewis, and J. R. R. Tolkien on the Human Condition*. Nashville: Broadman.

—. 2007. "*English Literature in the Sixteenth Century*: C.S. Lewis as a Literary Historian." *C.S. Lewis: Life, Works, Legacy*. Ed. Bruce Edwards. London: Praeger: 4:143-62.

—. 2012. *Inklings of Reality: Essays toward a Christian Philosophy of Letters*. 2nd ed. Lynchburg: Lantern Hollow Press.

—. 2004. "A Larger World: C.S. Lewis on Christianity and Literature." *Mythlore*, 24:2 (Summer 2004): 45-57.

—. 2007. "'The Mind Is its Own Place': Satan's Philosophy and the Modern Dilemma." *The Journal of the Georgia Philological Association* 2: 20-34.

—. 2012. *Reflections from Plato's Cave: Essays in Evangelical Theology*. Lynchburg: Lantern Hollow Press.

Wordsworth, Dorothy. 1997. *Recollections of a Tour Made in Scotland*. Carol Kyros Walker, ed. New Haven: Yale University Press.

Wordsworth, Jonathan, M.H. Abrams, and Stephen Gill. eds. 1979. *The Prelude 1799, 1805, 1850.* New York: Norton.